Escape

—

to Joy

With our love
Geeco

Geeco Publishing

First Published Amazon Kindle 2023

www.geecopublishing.com

ISBN: 978 1 7391073 7 6

Also published by Geeco

Enjoy In Joy

&

A Simple Way

Tradition 12

"Anonymity is the spiritual foundation of all our traditions, ever reminding us to place principles before personalities."

This book has been created by the joint efforts of the members of Geeco, and we are equal creators. We offer it to you from our collective name Geeco.

You can communicate with us at geeco909@gmail.com

If you enjoy the messages in this book, please help us to get them out there by leaving a review on Amazon.

Enjoy

January 1

Struggle

You drown not by falling into a river, but by staying submerged in it.

Paulo Coelho

You see someone drowning. What do you do? Dive in? Throw something? Watch pathetically?

Okay, let's make it easier for you. You're in a swimming pool, and you see someone... struggling. What do you do? Are they really struggling or just fooling around? Is there a lifeguard? Or do you just swim over and start helping?

Surely, it should be easy. We should know what to do. But if we've never been in this situation before? Then it's more complicated. We can hardly blame ourselves if they drown, can we?

But let's move on from them. (Let's assume they lived happily ever after.)

You, me, we are drowning, not in water, but in the world, at home, at work, in our lives.

What do we do? Are we ashamed to ask for help? Are we already too overwhelmed by it all to be able to reach out?

Okay, come back a bit. We aren't overwhelmed (yet), but things are not good. Do we swim further out?

If we cannot find a way to explain our need for help, then things will almost certainly get worse. Let's be brave, have courage and take action much sooner rather than too late.

Being in a state of confusion is a self-torture.

Sukant Ratnakar

January 2

Resilience

Sticks and stones may break my bones, but words will never hurt me.

English Proverb

Oh dear, Oh dear, Oh dear.

In the playground, red-faced, bitten lip, tear tracked across a grubby cheek, big breath in, as we desperately want to believe it.

Oh dear.

And maybe at that moment, it does help?

But later?

In all honesty, it's people's words that damage us the most. We store them away to chop ourselves up with later, at moments of weakness.

We want to learn to reject, discard, and destroy the negative things people say to and/or about us. We want to refuse to accept them and replace them in our minds with the positive.

We are not less than and want to know that we are so much more than we think. We want to be proud to be ourselves, and we want to love ourselves.

I believe if you'll just stand up and go, life will open up for you.

Tina Turner

January 3

Forgiveness

Reject your sense of injury and the injury itself disappears.

Marcus Aurelius

Somebody stuck a sticker on my car yesterday, complaining about my parking.

I presume it must have been one of my neighbours. But if they object to my parking, why can't they speak to me about it rather than slap a sticker on my car? Floods of revenge and retaliation thoughts swept through me. (I am, after all, human.)

I spoke to some friends about it because I know the importance of letting things out.

And this morning, one of the books I read reminded me that everything that is not love is a cry for help.

Looking at their attack as a cry for help completely changes it. It changes me.

Yes, the wound is still raw. Yes, it still hurts a little. But it's becoming a fading memory.

I'm so grateful that I don't live in their head.

I have peace.

It's not an easy journey to get to a place where you forgive people, But it is such a powerful place because it frees you.

Tyler Perry

January 4

Thoughts

*The one thing we can never get enough of is love. And the
one thing we never give enough of is love.*

Henry Miller

Despite all the hype about multi-tasking, we can, in fact,
only think one thing at a time.

Which is wonderful.

Because if we are thinking a negative, fearful, hateful or
angry thought, we can change it by thinking about something
else.

'It's not that easy!' you cry. 'You try!'

'Actually, it is.'

Start thinking about love, peace, or serenity.

Of course, the negative thought may spiral back in, but
we can loop straight out of it.

Thinking negative things hurts us, not others.

*Everything can be taken from a man, but one thing: the last
of the human freedoms – to choose one's attitude in any
given set of circumstances, to choose one's own way.*

Viktor E Frankl

Sorry

Never ruin an apology with an excuse.

Benjamin Franklin

Change his mind. Tell him you're sorry you grilled his shorts. That you're sorry you've got ice running through your veins.

C C Hunter

'I'm sorry.'

Don't insult the other person with 'I'm sorry, but...' or some lame excuse.

I'm sorry is meaningless unless it encompasses some new behaviour. If you're going to do it again, you might as well say, 'I'm sorry you didn't like it. Get used to it.'

Being a frail, mortal human, you may accidentally do it a second time. But that's it. Three strikes, and you're out.

Do it a third time, and don't embarrass the world with an 'I'm sorry'. You aren't sorry. You may be sorry for yourself. Sorry you are such a useless piece of dog ****, but you clearly are not sorry enough about how you affect the other person.

So don't insult them with your lies.

Change.

It's always too late for sorries, but I appreciate the sentiment.

Neil Gaiman

January 6

Storms

It matters not how strait the gate,
How charged with punishments the scroll,
I am the master of my fate:
I am the captain of my soul.

William Ernest Henley

Life happens. Again and again.

But we are not like tumbleweeds, blown by the whim of the wind.

We are more like a sailor at the helm of his boat, steering his way across the sea, using the wind and the sails to change his yacht's course.

He can do nothing about the weather. He has to accept being becalmed or battling in a raging storm. He can only guide himself through it.

One of the troubles is that we rant at the storm, do battle with it, and allow it to defeat us. If, instead, we accept the next thing that life throws at us, we can control our reactions. We can steer our way through it. We can face it with love and acceptance. Secure in the knowledge that it will change. Storms blow themselves out.

They pass.

When you come out of the storm, you won't be the same person who walked in. That's what this storm's all about.

Haruki Murakami

Life isn't about waiting for the storm to pass... It's about learning to dance in the rain.

Vivian Greene

Moving On

She laughed when I tried to tell her
Hello only ends in goodbye.

Rodriguez

We often want things to last forever without giving any real thought to what forever might mean.

Especially the first blossoms of love. We want, we imagine, and we fantasize that they will last forever. Or perhaps we cannot bear to consider their ending.

And our relationships with our parents, children, and siblings also come with a dollop of forever?

But consider the quote: 'Hello only ends in goodbye.'

If we acknowledge that. If we realise this truth, then what we are experiencing, or clinging to changes.

Accepting that everything ends, lessens the intensity of the fear that hides behind our clinging and our longing. It gives us space to live with a little more elegance.

It is liberating.

I rewrote the ending to 'Farewell to Arms', the last page of it, thirty-nine times before I was satisfied.

Ernest Hemingway

It's much easier to not know things sometimes. Things change and friends leave. And life doesn't stop for anybody.

Stephen Chbosky

Prayer

Lord, make me a channel of thy peace
That where there is hatred, I may bring love

Francis of Assisi

Do you know Francis of Assisi's prayer? He lived a thousand years ago, and I think it is one of the most amazing things ever written. I say it with meaning every day. I truly recommend it. If we were only to achieve a fraction of it, it would be life changing.

It ends with, 'It is by forgiving that one is forgiven. It is by dying that one awakens to eternal life.'

It seems incredible that someone living a thousand years ago believed that death led to eternal life. It seems amazing that anyone ever believed that. And it seems strange that I should be amazed when it is what I believe.

But there you are, we are strange, no escaping from that.

You don't have a soul. You are a soul. You have a body.

C S Lewis

January 9

Oneness

*To not be optimistic about the human race, would be a
disregard of the power of the Spirit who created All.*

Martin Suarez

When we stop viewing people as individuals and realise
that we are all one, it changes everything.

When we are one, there is no one worse than us or better
than us. No one. For we are one.

Even the most atrocious things people do, if processed
with the understanding that we are one, can change how we
perceive it. We can say, 'Forgive them as I forgive myself, for
we are one.'

The only way to achieve peace and harmony within
ourselves and the world is to accept, forgive and love.

Forgiveness and love unites us with peace.

No act of kindness, no matter how small, is ever wasted.

Aesop

The only path wide enough for us all is love.

Kamand Kojouri

January 10

Ego

My ego mind – my own self-hatred masquerading as self-love – would point me always in the direction of fear, luring me toward the blaming thought, the attack or defence, the perception of guilt in myself or others.

Marianne Williamson

There are two voices in our heads, the ego and the inner voice of love, peace and calm.

They create our thoughts. They are the source of our thoughts. And every thought, idea, behaviour, and anything we do or say that is not loving or kind comes from our ego.

And every word, deed or behaviour that others produce that is not loving comes from their ego.

Our ego does not love us. It wants to control us. It does not want us to succeed. It certainly does not want us to be loving.

Our other voice, the quiet, gentle inner voice, wants us to give and experience peace and love. It wants others to enjoy this, too. It can help lead us to harmony within ourselves and the world.

We choose which voice to listen to.

We choose.

Always.

Ego says, 'Once everything falls into place, I'll find peace.'
Spirit says, 'Find your peace, and then everything will fall into place.'

Marianne Williamson

January 11

Burdens

*It is dreadful when something weighs on your mind, not to
have a soul to unburden yourself to. You know what I
mean. I tell my piano the things I used to tell you.*

Frédéric Chopin

So important to be unburdened. Very important.

I think so many people wake up in the morning and
instantly search for the things that were dragging them down
yesterday. Then they haul this grungy old sack out from
under their bed. They fill it with the biggest boulders of
resentment, anger, fear, being put upon and anything else
that catches their eye.

They heave the sack over their shoulder and stomp off,
operating at perhaps 75% of their potential.

If you have a boulder, bring it out. Look at it. Share it.
Discard it.

Live

Enjoy.

*You do not have to unburden your soul for everyone: it will
be enough if you do that for those you love.*

Albert Camus

*The road to success is dotted with many tempting parking
spaces.*

Will Rogers

Love

*It felt so amazing to be alive, I could never think of
anything else.*

Marty Rubin

I was talking to my son the other day, you know how one
does, about being in love.

And we decided that being in love with someone happens
because they make you feel totally alive.

Alive and blessed.

*How beautiful it is when one lives completely and not just
with part of oneself. When one is full to the rim and calm
because there is nothing more to get in.*

Erich Maria Remarque

Perception

The truth is, unless you let go, unless you forgive yourself, unless you forgive the situation, unless you realise that the situation is over, you cannot move forward.

Steve Maraboli

Anything, no everything unacceptable that has happened in our lives, can create disharmony in us now if we have not truly moved on from it. If you still feel wronged because Jimmy pushed you over in the playground when you were five, or as Wayne Dyer said, 'Because your mother loved your sister more than she loved you', it is damaging you now.

And the same goes for what is happening in your life now. If someone got promoted over you, or your Mother-in-law insists on giving you things you wouldn't even take to a charity shop, your resentment will destroy you for as long as you allow it to.

We have two perspectives that we see the world through – either with our ego or our inner being. The ego creates angst, our inner being, peace and love.

We can choose whether to feel peace and love or agitation and madness.

Anger begets more anger, and forgiveness and love lead to more forgiveness and love.

Mahavira

January 14

Inner Child

Caring for your inner child has a powerful and surprisingly quick result: Do it and the child heals.

Martha Beck

We all have an inner child, and most of us neglect our child. We don't even think about it.

Have you ever or do you ever feel less good, happy, whole than you would like? Come to that, do you ever feel (to use a technical expression) like shit?

If any of those bad things happen, or we are just clenching our teeth for no apparent reason, then there is something simple and life-changing that we can do.

Go inside, into your body and being, and pick up your inner child. Hug and bathe your child with love.

There, isn't that amazing?

Could there be anything easier to do?

It sounds corny, but I've promised my inner child that never again will I ever abandon myself for anything or anyone else.

Wynonna Judd

When childhood dies, its corpses are called adults.

Brian Aldiss

When I grow up, I want to be a little boy.

Joseph Heller

Co-dependence

Your mother doesn't need a diagnosis for you to determine that your relationship is unhealthy.

Diane Metcalf

Co-dependence. I didn't even know what that meant. For years, for most of my early life, my happiness was totally dependent on other people. As I moved into my teenage years (God help all teenagers), I started to think I was in love... (infatuation is more accurate). I realised the insanity of allowing my happiness, peace of mind, and enjoyment to be ruled by whether they 'did' or 'didn't', do, 'this', or 'that'...

I discovered codependence.

And I suspect most of us have at least a trace of that. We have hopes and expectations about the future and how our interactions with others will make it 'good' or 'bad'.

Letting go of that, or even realising we are doing it, changes it.

The only person who can make you happy is yourself!

Do yourself a favour and enjoy your life.

Always do the right thing, despite the games someone else is playing.

Tracy A Malone

There is never anything to change but our own perspective.

Karen Casey

January 16

Doing

Laziness is nothing more than the habit of resting before you get tired.

Jules Renard

If we feel tired and can't think clearly, our ego is in control. It creates thoughts and feelings that stop us from being free, present and in the moment.

Yes, there may be times when we genuinely need to sleep and rest, which is fine. But there are also times when exhaustion zaps us, takes our energy away, and encourages us to become a blob that needs to give up. The ego doesn't want us to face the reality of the task at hand, so it seduces us into giving up.

It happened to me twenty minutes ago, so I know what I'm talking about. And rather than give in to it and collapse, I went to my other voice, my inner being, handed my life over, and here I am scribbling away.

So much better than being a blob.

You will find peace not by trying to escape your problems, but by confronting them courageously. You will find peace not in denial, but in victory.

J Donald Walters

January 17

Training

*The most important part of education is proper training in
the nursery.*

Plato

He who sweats more in training bleeds less in war.

Greek Proverb

The way people become good at what they do is through
training. Think of sports teams, soldiers, actors (to pick a
few), and you will realise that when confronted with a major
challenge, they know what to do. They have spent hours
training for this kind of event when the pressure was not
real.

And in fact, that is a good way to view your life. Realise
that the situations you find yourself in now are just training
exercises. So that when, or if, you meet a challenge, you'll
have the tools to cope with it.

Life is just a training exercise. It is not important. You are
just an apprentice learning as you go. Nobody expects you to
be perfect. Relax. You'll get through it. It doesn't matter.
Keep it simple.

*On the mountains of truth you can never climb in vain:
either you will reach a point higher up today, or you will be
training your powers so that you will be able to climb
higher tomorrow.*

Friedrich Nietzsche

Life

Everything has its drawbacks, as the man said when his mother-in-law died, and they came down upon him for the funeral expenses.

Jerome K. Jerome

Let's face it, we have to take the rough with the smooth. It is not a conspiracy. 'They' are not out to get us. Life happens.

If (or when) we accept that and just allow ourselves the freedom to journey through our day with as much elegance as we can, everything is so much easier.

We cannot control events or people. We can do our part and move on.

And we want to enjoy our part as much as it is possible. If we do not enjoy it, this is because we are taking everything too seriously.

I can't sit still and see another man slaving and working. I want to get up and superintend, and walk round with my hands in my pockets, and tell him what to do. It is my energetic nature. I can't help it.

Jerome K Jerome

Addiction

*Whether you sniff it, smoke it, eat it or shove it up your ass
the result is the same: addiction.*

William S Burroughs

*Every form of addiction is bad, no matter whether the
narcotic be alcohol or morphine or idealism,*

Carl Jung

In Alcoholics Anonymous, they say that it is the first drink that does the damage. The newcomer says, 'No, it's the sixth, tenth, or the fourteenth. If I could stop, then it would not be a problem.' And the people in AA say, 'No, it's the first one. If you don't have the first one, none of the others would follow.'

And this is true of all addictions. If we didn't take the first chocolate, start playing the computer game, go on Facebook, or take the first line of cocaine, then it wouldn't be a problem.

Similarly, if we don't do our exercise today, or eat well, or sleep well, it is much harder to get back into the habit of doing the good thing.

It's the first one that does the damage.

Beware.

*We are addicted to our thoughts. We cannot change
anything if we cannot change our thinking.*

Santosh Kalwar

Reality is just a crutch for people who can't handle drugs.

Robin Williams

January 20

Respect

It would be too easy to say that I feel invisible. Instead, I feel painfully visible, and entirely ignored.

David Levithan

I wheeled a friend into a restaurant, and everyone was very helpful. We settled at a table. The waiter came over, asked me what I wanted to drink and then said, 'What would he like?'

How can it be that people assume because you are disabled or a child or old that you cannot speak and decide for yourself?

It is like shouting your language at a foreigner because somehow you think that slow, shouted words will find their way into their brain.

And I suspect that even if we do not do any of the above, there are moments in our lives when we treat people in some 'special' way or 'disregard' someone because, at a core level in our being, we perceive them as different.

I cannot, at this moment, think of a single incident when I have done that, and yet I am absolutely certain that I have.

And if I do not guard myself against it, I will do it again. I am, after all, just a human being.

What's worse than being hated is being ignored, because it's like you don't exist at all and your presence is nothing.

Anurag Prakash Ray

Stones make no splash on a frozen lake.

Steven Erikson

January 21

Pain

These pains you feel are messengers.

Listen to them.

Rumi

So often, we suppress our emotional pain, ignoring it as best we can. Or we indulge in one of our addictions to take our minds off it. And maybe, at this moment, that is all we can do.

But our pains are there for a reason. As toothache tells us, we have a problem with a tooth, and if we do not do something about it, it will worsen.

Our mental disquiet is also telling us that there is something in our lives that we need to address. If we do not, the decay will only increase.

So talk about it with your trusted friend. Write letters to yourself about it. Explore and uncover it. Have the courage to take steps to change it before it engulfs you.

Act as if what you do makes a difference.

IT DOES.

William James

Secrecy

The more you don't want to be like your parents, the more you will resemble them.

Yong Kang Chan

I was brought up within an aura of secrecy. We never said anything that would 'let the side down' or expose the frailties of our family. Nobody must ever know that my parents were not perfect or that my brother was stupid.

We lived in a make-believe bubble. When I saw that other people's lives were full of troubles, I assumed that there was something terribly wrong with them because I had reached the stage of believing that the lie I lived in was real, that it was the truth.

We were taught, 'Don't ever tell people what is happening. They will take advantage of you.'

I believed it completely, as did my inner child, who fought for years to keep everything secret.

It is such a relief to have finally discarded this insanity. Well, for the most part, anyway. Sometimes, my inner child takes control and snaps my mouth shut, lest I be found out.

It is so much more comfortable to live with openness and honesty.

The man who can keep a secret may be wise, but he is not half as wise as the man with no secret to keep.

Edgar Watson Howe

Secrecy, once accepted, becomes an addiction.

Edward Teller

January 23

Being

Be here now

Ram Dass

Be here now.

Be in your body. Feel it. Feel the air on your face. Experience your breath. Sink into whatever is supporting your weight.

Be.

Smell. Taste. Touch. Listen. Feel.

Let the world stop.

Even if only for a fleeting...

It is different.

Do it often.

It will reward you.

> *To him who has had the experience, no explanation is necessary, to him who has not, none is possible.*

> *Ram Dass*

Control

Control leaves no room for trust

Glennon Doyle

If only they'd do this! Or that! If only I had control over them. Then everything would be, well, if not perfect, at least so much better.

But hang on a moment. If I were able to have control over them, then it would follow because of nature, creation, God, the universe, balance, call it what you will, that if I had control over them, then they would have control over me.

They would be able to decide what I did! How I behaved!

So, think carefully when you wish others would do things the way you would like them to.

True love is built on free will and free choice, not control and manipulation.

Ken Poirot

Ego

Only when you've truly had enough suffering in your life, are you able to say, 'I don't need it anymore'.

Eckhart Tolle

Our ego wants us to suffer, that is how it controls us. It takes us back into the black of the past or the bleakness awaiting us in the future. It does not want us to be in the present moment, whole and together.

We want to learn to live in the present as much as we can. The present is the only reality. The past and the future do not exist, except in our minds.

There is one thing I enjoy doing by way of a snub to the ego. When I think about the past or the future, instead of going into the sorrow, disappointment, pain, fear, disaster elements that are offered, I think of good, happy times with joy. I imagine everything going wonderfully. And I smile.

Your soul knows the shortest, safest route to your true destiny. Why is your ego behind the wheel?

Anthon St. Maarten

Forgiveness

Forgive them even if they are not sorry.

Julian Casablancas

When we do not forgive, we are planting resentments in ourselves.

Even a little sigh of disappointment is a resentment.

And the resentment damages us. Not them. Not the world. Just us.

And okay, a sigh may not be much of a bother. (Apparently.)

But it is a straw. Yet another straw that we are adding to our back. And it is only a question of time before our back finally snaps.

So, forgive them.

If for no other reason than the selfish one of keeping our house clean. However, if that is how you view it, you have not really forgiven them.

Forgive them completely. Give/send them love.

Forgiveness is a gift you give yourself.

Suzanne Somers

Touch

Never touch a butterfly's wing with your finger.

Sidonie Gabrielle Colette

I was working on a house in Wales with a friend. He fell off a ladder, and I rushed to see if I could help.

He screamed, 'Don't touch me!' So, I didn't.

He explained later that, in his experience, the body needs time to regroup and become whole again after an accident. If anyone touched him before that process was completed, their touch removed his personal power, and his recovery took far longer.

Since then, I have stopped people from touching me when I've had an accident. And I can feel my body gathering itself together, and start the healing process. It is as if the pieces of the puzzle are slotting into one another.

I only mention this in case there is some truth in it. However, I believe that once the regrouping has happened, being touched with love can enhance the healing process.

Although not everyone is blessed with a healing touch, our touch can be a source of healing and blessing for others, especially when accompanied by a brief prayer.

Tom Cowan

Love

Letting go doesn't mean that you don't care about someone any more. It's just realising that the only person you really have control over, is yourself.

Deborah Reber

True love is letting go.

True love is the gift of freedom, of accepting the other person as they are.

When we begin our journey of love – closeness, intimacy, and oneness rule the emotions. And so often, we are unable to move on from that. We are unable to accept the changes in the relationship.

True love is the gift of freedom. It does not make demands. True love is not physical. It does not have expectations.

True love is when the God in me and the God in you embrace. If our physical togetherness ends, our egos may create pain and suffering, but if there is true love, our Gods will rejoice in the lives of one another because they are one.

Love one another but make no bond of love.

Kahlil Gibran

January 29

Judgement

Successful people are successful because they never judge anyone, even after knowing them completely.

Anuj Jasani

Most people's default setting is to be judgemental, and even if it is not as prevalent as that, we nearly all tend to look on life and others with judgement.

The opposite of being judgemental is to be compassionate and loving.

The world is a far more appealing place when we view it with love and compassion. It is softer. And the immediate benefit to us is that we also feel better about ourselves.

The more we wean ourselves off judgement and onto a diet of love and compassion, the better our life becomes.

When the power of love overcomes the love of power, the world will know peace.

Jimi Hendrix

January 30

Honesty

Stop thinking and end your problems.

Lao Tzu

A friend of mine, a priest, who is one of the most caring, magical people I know, had a call to say that his car mechanic had had a heart attack.

His first thought was, 'Has he finished my car?'

He told me this because he wanted me to realise that he, too, was human.

Isn't it extraordinary how easily, quickly and instinctively we dive into 'me'?

Into how will this affect me? How long will this take? Is this going to make me late? What will people think? Endless bits of personal worries. I couldn't begin to list them all, there would be room for nothing else in this book.

I guess it's called being human. Taking care of number one. And we should not feel bad about it, everyone does it. But we can choose how we act upon it.

The essence of the independent mind lies not in what it thinks, but in how it thinks.

Christopher Hitchens

January 31

Suffering

Life is pain, highness. Anyone who says differently is selling something.

William Goldman

We suffer. We suffer because things are not right. And we want them mended. We want perfection.

Of course, we have no idea that we want perfection. The very idea of perfection is absurd. We know that. And certainly do not think that that is why we suffer.

No, but we do want some things in our lives fixed. At some level, we are saying, 'Please, just snap your fingers and take away or fix my challenges. All of them, but start with...'

What do you want to be fixed first, your partner, your kids, your eating/drinking/drugging, your job, the trash collectors, your neighbour's dog, or the traffic on the road?

Oh, and how about yourself while you're at it? Your self-image, your body, your fears, your anger, and your inner pain?

So that is why we suffer. And as long as we are fighting, it will continue. Most people do not honestly want to stop suffering. They will only change when the pain becomes intense enough.

So, the pain is a friend. When we accept that, we may be able to begin to change and enjoy our lives.

We must embrace pain and burn it as fuel for our journey.

Kenji Miyazawa

Life tried to crush her, but only succeeded in creating a diamond.

John Mark Green

Keep
it
simple

Behaviour

*We're waiting for a glance or a word, some
acknowledgement that we are here.*

Jeet Thayil

We all need acknowledgement. We need to be wanted and to be appreciated. To be recognised. It is a basic demand that our psyche makes to enable us to feel whole.

As we give, so do we receive.

Everyone wants and needs acknowledgement. And while we cannot make any specific person acknowledge us, if they choose not to, we can increase the quantity and quality we receive by consciously increasing our acknowledgement of them.

We want to spend that little bit of extra time and energy to honestly give others our attention, thoughts and love.

When we express our gratitude it grows.

Richie Norton

February 2

Masks

You wear a mask for so long, you forget who you were beneath it.

Alan Moore

Behind the mask of ice that people wear, there beats a heart of fire.

Paulo Coelho

We drag around an old trunk filled with the masks we've accumulated during our lives. The 'I'm fine' mask, the 'I'm the best Dad/Mum', the 'I'm such a success', the 'I like you', the 'I'm always right', the 'Please don't realise how insecure I'm feeling' masks.

Maybe none of those apply to you, but I bet, if you're honest, you can easily think of a handful that do.

(How about the 'I'm a really good member of my religion?' mask.)

We started our collection as little children and have continued to add to it. We wear them because we feel inadequate and fear others will realise we are.

In truth, none of us are inadequate. We are on a journey through challenges that we will continue to have until we have discovered the message they hold for us.

And by daring to accept who we are and by admitting it to the world, we will find that we can move forward with far greater ease than we imagined.

Sometimes, it's not the people who change, it's the mask that falls off.

Haruki Murakami

Tear off the mask. Your face is glorious.

Rumi

February 3

Action

Don't be fooled by the calendar. There are only as many days in the year as you make use of. One man gets only a week's value out of a year, while another man gets a full year's value out of a week.

Charles Richards

Have you got five minutes?

I mean, do you ever find yourself with five minutes?

You've just finished something and don't need to start the next thing for five minutes.

What do you do?

Plonk down?

Fill them with some unimportant activity.

Okay, let's ask another question, do you have a project you'd like to achieve that you haven't started because you never have the time or spend very little on because you're always so busy?

If you swooped up all the odd five minutes you have here and there during the day and put them into your project, might it go ahead?

Or, when you have five minutes, rather than just vegging, if you spend three of them meditating, do you think everything would be better?

(I know it would, but don't take my word for it, prove it to yourself.)

Time is more valuable than money. You can get more money, but you cannot get more time.

Jim Rohn

Criticism

Remember, you have been criticising yourself for years, and it hasn't worked. Try approving of yourself and see what happens.

Louise Hay

That really says it all, doesn't it?

People ask you for criticism, but they only want praise.

W Somerset Maugham

February 5

Doing Good

How far that little candle throws his beams!
So shines a good deed in a weary world.

William Shakespeare – The Merchant of Venice

When I was a kid, I was a Boy Scout, and one of the things we did was a good deed every day.

However, now that I'm older (a little), I still do my best to do a good deed every day. At the very least, smiling whenever possible in the hopes of getting a smile back counts as a good deed.

Or I consider what I can do for a work colleague or neighbour.

It is taking my mind off the 'great me' and onto the other people in the world. It feels good.

Enjoy.

If you do one good deed, your reward usually is to be set to do another and harder and better one.

C S Lewis

February 6

Self-Doubt

Accept that you are enough. You don't need to be anything you are not.

Wayne Dyer

You were given this life because you are strong enough to live it.

Robin Sharma

I am enough.

You are enough.

It's so easy to go through our day (our life even) finding fault with ourselves.

And even if we do not pick out specific faults to spear ourselves with, we find subtle shortcomings in ourselves.

Maybe only self-doubting or self-questioning in the back of our minds.

While we assume that most people are doing better than we are.

Of course, we may even travel along secure in our knowledge that we are better than anyone else.

But if we look at that closely, could it be a shield we've created to stop ourselves from acknowledging our failings?

You alone are enough. You have nothing to prove to anybody.

Maya Angelou

February 7

Motivation

It is amazing what you can accomplish if you do not care who gets the credit.

Harry S Truman

Be ashamed to die until you have won some victory for humanity.

Horace Mann

What do you want?

Looking into the future, deep future, what will make you happy? What will make you complete?

What, when you take off your slippers for the last time, do you want to think of with joy and pride?

What are you doing to make that a reality?

If what you have done yesterday still looks big to you, you haven't done much today.

Mikhail S Gorbachev

The difference between ordinary and extraordinary is that little extra.

Jimmy Johnson

February 8

Sleep

And it irritated me beyond all measure that a thought so enormous and ludicrous should return when my logic had dismissed it.

Clark Ashton Smith

Those thoughts that pop or explode into our minds as we move towards sleep. All those things we need to do or haven't done.

The best way to deal with them is to have an **everything to-do list** and put **everything on it**, so when we think 'Must call Anne' or 'Must be more confident' we can say to ourselves, I don't need to think about that, it's on the list.

And at that moment, ask yourself, 'Is there anything I can do about it now?'

If there isn't anything you can do, then say, 'I'm not going to think about it until the morning,' and drop the thought out of your mind.

It is an excellent idea to listen to a meditation as you go to sleep, and if you don't, then concentrate on your breathing.

Saying 'Sleep' on every out-breath also helps.

Tired minds don't plan well. Sleep first, plan later.

Walter Reisch

Sleep is that golden chain that ties health and our bodies together.

Thomas Dekker

Happiness

Happiness consists of a solid faith, good health and a bad memory.

Clare Boothe Luce

There are moments when we are happy, and it flows through every part of our being without thought. But sadly, those moments of unfettered joy are rare.

Most of the time, we bumble through our day, neither happy nor sad, just being.

Then there are those days when, even if we don't wake up feeling depressed or overwhelmed, it creeps up and envelopes us later. (And interestingly, by and large, we assume that this doesn't happen to others, just to us.)

There are two things to consider here. The first is what we give to the world, we receive. So, if we can make an effort to give others peace, love, and acceptance, they will be returned to us.

The second is that people, possessions, and things cannot make us happy. We have to do happy within ourselves.

We have a choice in how we react to our inner feelings and voices.

If we say, 'God, I feel depressed,' we can follow that into depression or say, 'No! I am not going to follow you.' And put a smile on our face.

It may not bring us instant happiness, but it will keep us out of the pit.

Happiness depends on ourselves.

Aristotle

A great obstacle to happiness is to expect too much happiness.

Bernard de Fontenelle

Home

A house is not a home.

Polly Adler

'A House is Not a Home' is an autobiography by Polly Adler, based on running her brothel in New York during the 1920s and 1930s.

And obviously, her house was not a home.

But it seems that many more people live in houses (not brothels, just houses) than live in homes.

A home is built with the heart, with love, with tiny acts of kindness.

A plastic or cardboard dwelling in a refugee camp can be more of a home than many of the comfortable houses in a city.

When we are surrounded by comfort, it is so easy to take things for granted. To expect things to be and people to behave the way we want.

It is so easy to lose sight of the people we live with. To assume that a peck on the cheek in the morning and a 'How was your day' in the evening (without listening to the reply) are all we need to do.

Wrong.

He is happiest, be he king or peasant, who finds peace in his home.

Johann Wolfgang von Goethe

Fear

Fear cuts deeper than swords.

George R R Martin

By and large, when we are with people, we imagine that they are okay. We do not think that they are fearful.

Yes, they may have some troubles, but we don't perceive them as having an inner core of fear.

I was at a meeting the other day with about a dozen people. We were talking about fear. And everyone said they suffered, at some level, from fear.

So perhaps, when we meet people whom we judge to be successful, easygoing, really together, we remember, 'This person has fear.'

We might then judge them and ourselves differently.

We could feel more 'equal to' rather than 'less' or 'better' than them.

Our whole interaction with them would be different.

Each of us must confront our own fears and must come face to face with them. How we handle our fears will determine where we go with the rest of our lives. To experience adventure or to be limited by the fear of it.

Judy Blume

February 12

Oneness

Invisible threads are the strongest ties.

Friedrich Nietzsche

Yesterday, I met a man for the third time in my life. The first time was over twenty years ago, the second about twelve and then again yesterday.

Our relationship has so much peace, understanding, and gentle joy, such oneness, a genuine soul mate.

He was about to go on a cruise, travelling to beautiful and exciting places. I asked him, of all the places he was going to, which was the one he was most looking forward to. 'Oh, seeing you.' He replied.

It is so awesome to have that kind of connection with anyone. It is so important to cherish it when we do and to remember it with joy.

Thank you.

Love is our true destiny. We do not find the meaning of life by ourselves alone – we find it with another.

Thomas Merton.

Peace

We're all just walking each other home.

Ram Dass

There is an ease to walking someone home or being accompanied as we return. No threats. No force. Just a relaxed togetherness.

This idea, very gently, very subtly, changes everything.

If all we are doing with each other is quietly walking home, how much more comfortable that is.

And if we do not relate to this feeling, it is because we are trying to get involved with things we have no control over anyway.

Let us change our perception. When we change our perception, the perception of everyone else changes too.

Let us walk peacefully home together and rejoice.

Do not go out there and seek quiet – Become it.

Meeta Ahluwalia

Being

Your emotions are the slaves to your thoughts, and you are the slave to your emotions.

Elizabeth Gilbert

We say, 'I'm in pain'. We do not say, 'I am pain'.

We are greater than the pain. The pain does not own us. It is simply part of us.

And although we may say, 'I'm depressed,' or 'I'm miserable', or even 'I'm happy', the important and missing part of any of those statements is, 'I feel...'

We have a choice about how we feel. Yes, we do.

We exist above all those feelings. We are greater than the feelings.

So, choose to ascend above them. And if you won't do that, then travel forward in your mind and know that in the future, they will have changed.

And there's a clue. Looking back over your life, you can see the changes and growth you've been through.

So, choose to feel okay or even better than that.

Between stimulus and response, there is a space. In that space is our power to choose our response. In our response lies our growth and our freedom.

Viktor E Frankl

February 15

Choices

*It is not the strongest or the most intelligent who will
survive but those who can best manage change.*

Charles Darwin

We are, on the whole, adaptable. Good at making the best
of the situation we are in.

There are times when we have virtually no choice in
what's happening, and we put up with things we dislike. Or,
we avoid rocking the boat because it feels uncomfortable,

The trouble with being too adaptable is that we find
ourselves just 'going along' with all kinds of things we do not
want to do. They don't all come at once. They are added one
at a time, so we hardly notice them increasing.

Until they finally overwhelm us, and we erupt like a kid
throwing its toys from the pram. It spells doom.

If we are to manage change, we want to do it calmly from
our inner being.

We want to discover how to alter things slowly and
elegantly. Alternatively, we want to allow ourselves to leave
the situation if that becomes our choice.

We are magnificent human beings. We were not sent here
to be enslaved.

*At some point, something or someone is going to disrupt
your entire life. Shouldn't it be you?*

Nicky Verd

Death

*'Time,' the Captain said, 'is not what you think.' He sat
down next to Eddie. 'Dying? Not the end of everything. We
think it is. But what happens on earth is only the beginning.'*

Mitch Albom

As we sit here (assuming you are sitting) in our bodies,
death can feel so real if we think about it.

Our death. And the death of others. The death of people
we've already lost. The future death of loved ones. It all
seems so heart-achingly real.

And yet, we are spirits in a body. We, the spirit, are the
ones who are experiencing this world, this life, this day. We,
the spirit, are the ones who see, taste, feel, love, laugh, and
exist, and the ones who do any negative shit too.

Our bodies are just vehicles. They are not us. Just as the
car we get in and drive is not us. We know this, and it is the
same with our bodies.

So death need have no power over us. We are alive.

Death was a friend, and sleep was Death's brother.

John Steinbeck

Teachers

Everybody's a teacher if you listen.

Doris Roberts

We are all teachers. We are teaching all the time, wherever we go. And we are all students as well.

It is important to remember that we teach by example. People learn by watching what we do rather than hearing what we say. If we are not doing it, why should they?

If our teaching fails, and they do not learn, it is not their fault. It is ours.

The blame does not lie with the student. It lies with the teacher.

Our method needs to be corrected.

If we cannot change them, we can always change ourselves.

If we choose to.

The art of teaching is the art of assisting discovery.

Mark Van Doren

February 18

Honesty

In my relationships with persons I have found that it does not help, in the long run, to act as though I were something I am not.

Carl Rogers

It is so easy to attempt to present ourselves in a better light. To hide bits and show other parts of ourselves that are only half-truths.

So much more rewarding for ourselves and others to dare to be open and honest.

If you do not tell the truth about yourself, you cannot tell it about other people.

Virginia Woolf

February 19

Judgement

Every day is judgement day. Always has been. Always will be.

Tom Robbins

We do not need to wait until judgement day to be judged. We do it to ourselves all the time. We create the hell or the heaven we choose to live in. We choose what we do or do not do today. We choose how we feel about it.

We decide whether we are going to continue to do it. We do not need anyone to tell us whether we are behaving well or not. We know.

We punish ourselves when we believe we have 'done wrong'.

We are our best buddy or our jailor and hangman.

Who are you going to choose to live with today?

I shall tell you a great secret, my friend. Do not wait for the last judgement – it takes place every day.

Albert Camus

Struggle

*It is exactly in tough times when we discover our full
potential, it allows our mind and body to push ourselves
beyond our limits.*

Leonardo Bonucci

Yes, people talk about troubles passing. But this one!?
No! No chance!

When you are really in it, totally in it, fighting on with
your last pieces of energy, the belief and hope that it will ever
end seems impossibly remote.

Yet still, you struggle on. The bog has long since
swallowed your gumboots, and now, with your naked,
bleeding feet, you still haul yourself forward into the
blackness.

However, now, looking back, you can hardly recall...

Life happens. Pain and struggle – solution, accept. Use
that quiet knowing to help you through the struggle.

Be silly not to, really.

Wouldn't it?

*Do not be concerned too much with what will happen.
Everything which happens will be good and useful for you.*

Epictetus

February 21

Laughter

Laugh, and the whole world laughs with you;

Weep, and you weep alone.

Ella Wheeler Wilcox

Of course, there are those ghastly moments when you laugh, a little too loudly perhaps, and no one else does. They turn and look at you as you pray for the earth to open and swallow you whole.

But, ha ha ha, leaving them aside, laughter and smiles are nectar to our souls. We cannot wait for others to start it. We want to be the cheerleaders ourselves. Giving and encouraging laughter wherever we go.

When things go wrong, taking them badly, with anger, frustration, and impatience, only makes them worse.

At that moment, if you're with others, it probably doesn't help to laugh, but looking on the situation lightheartedly makes finding the solution far more likely.

And the sooner you can laugh at it, the better.

Life doesn't imitate art, it imitates bad television.

Woody Allen

Nothing matters very much, and very few things matter at all.

Arthur Balfour

Gratitude

A hundred times a day, I remind myself that my inner and outer lives are based on the labours of other people, living and dead and that I must exert myself in order to give in the same measure as I have received and am still receiving.

Albert Einstein

There are many things in our lives that we take for granted. Even a hundred years ago, things that now seem normal to us were impossible.

We can drive or fly hundreds or thousands of miles without thinking about it. We can buy virtually anything we want. We can change careers.

We want to spend a little time in awe and gratitude for all the marvels of our lives.

We are not at war or being attacked by our neighbour.

We have freedoms that were unimaginable for our ancestors.

Do not squander your privileges.

Give thanks for them.

You never know the worth of water till the well is dry.

Thomas Fuller

What you leave behind is not what is engraved in stone monuments but what is woven into the lives of others.

Pericles

Stopping

*In the silence behind what can be heard lies the answers we
have been searching for, for so long.*

Andreas Fransson

When did you last listen to the silence? Lose yourself in
listening?
It does not require that you stop doing.
And most of us are not very good at stopping.
But do it.
Stop.
Stand, sit or lie down and listen.
Even in a silent place, there is so much to listen to.
Not to mention your soul.

Listen to the silence. It has so much to say.

Rumi

Change

When we are no longer able to change a situation – we are challenged to change ourselves.

Viktor E Frankl

How long do we take to decide, to realise and accept that we cannot change a situation?

How long do we allow it to have power over us when, in reality, we know that we cannot do anything about it?

Of course, we have a stubborn, in-built resistance to changing ourselves.

We know that changing ourselves requires effort, so we dig our heels in and cling to the same old for as long as possible.

However, I know from personal experience that when I finally let go and make changes, I instantly feel so much better, lighter, and freer, and I wonder why I didn't do it ages ago.

One day your life will flash before your eyes. Make sure it's worth watching.

Gerard Way

Death

Don't cry because it's over, smile because it happened.

Dr Seuss

The mother of a friend of mine is dying. I talked about it with a friend, who said, 'Ah yes, she's reclaiming her freedom.'

If, as I believe, we are souls in a human body, this makes complete sense.

And, I think, alters the whole concept of death.

They are reclaiming their freedom, so surely we want to feel happy for them.

For life and death are one, even as the river and the sea are one.

Kahlil Gibran

As soon as you realise it was a gift, you'll be free.

Maxime Lagacé

Thinking

To think too much is a disease.

Fyodor Dostoevsky

Only about two per cent of one per cent of our thoughts deserve to be taken seriously.

Mokokoma Mokhonoana

Oh yes, thinking, I remember. Yup, it's a bit like swimming in porridge in a bowl with high sides.

Round and round we go. Nowhere, burning endless energy. Such turmoil.

It is the ego, of course. Just having a good laugh at our expense, creating problems on top of problems.

If we go inside ourselves, into the now, into our inner being, and bathe there for a fraction, all the thinking disappears. There is gentle peace.

But beware, the ego waits at the door, a coiled spring, ready to leap. But we do not need to let it. It is our life. Not the egos.

Thinking too much leads to paralysis by analysis. It's important to think things through, but many use thinking as a means of avoiding action.

Robert Herjavec

Soon you will be dead and none of it will matter.

Marcus Aurelius

Relationships

*If I behave as though this is a completely normal situation,
then maybe it will be...*

Sophie Kinsella

My in-laws have just spent a week with us. Which was fine. Good even.

However...

When our order is disturbed, we change our behaviours. We do and say things that are not quite 'us'. And it requires an 'effort'.

Of course, the amount of effort required varies, depending on who or what the circumstances are.

And when the in-laws leave, we can all breathe a sigh of relief and go back to normal.

Or can we? What is normal?

The truth is that as we go through our day, we are constantly being required, forced, or obliged to behave in a certain way. And we do that quite willingly, most of the time.

It is important to realise this. And allow ourselves from time to time to recentre into who we truly are.

It makes living far more manageable.

*May you live a life as holy and as perfect as you pretend it
to be in Facebook.*

Maria Nieves

*I talk about a life that I pretend to live, and you ask me
what I'm talking about. But when I finally tell, you regret
finding out.*

Harley Mei Kent

February 28

Living

I was dead and now I live
You took my hand

Harold Pinter – Poem –'To My Wife'

I hope that someone has taken your hand during your life.

I think we are dead until someone does.

I think that we can, if we are lucky, give life to another by taking their hand.

When that happens, both are truly blessed.

If you're not sure, keep hunting.

The payoff is beyond this world. The payoff is unconditional.

You are my life
And so I live

Harold Pinter – Poem –'To My Wife'

Compassion

More smiling, less worrying. More compassion, less judgement. More blessed, less stressed. More love, less hate.

Roy T Bennett

There are people in our lives we feel naturally warm towards and love. But we have no strong feelings about most people we interact with.

If we think of the people we meet with compassion, it changes how we view them. It softens everything.

Compassion is born out of love.

And if we can allow our being to fill with love. To fill us with an aura of love that goes out and encompasses the people we are with. It changes everything.

And if you think I couldn't do that with 'him' not after...

Please remember that the aura of love is not involved with the individual or anything that has happened.

It is not judgemental. It simply surrounds whomever you are with.

It changes all interactions.

If we have no peace, it is because we have forgotten that we belong to each other.

Mother Teresa

Enjoy

sharing

it

with

someone

else

Judgement

I hate stupid people. They should have to wear signs that just say, 'I'm stupid'.

Bill Engvall

I'm sitting looking out at my river. (Please note the 'my' – I don't own it but think of it as mine. It is, after all, outside my window.)

A man comes along with his two sons (say, 8 and 11), and the boys throw branches into the water. Some branches are far too big for them, so Dad heaves them in, and they mindlessly saunter off.

It is interesting, isn't it, how my mind makes them into stupid hooligans. Were they actually doing any harm? Is it that I do not want them to enjoy themselves?

Who is suffering here? Certainly not them.

No, I'm creating, bathing in negativity, and poisoning myself with it. Why on earth would I choose to do that?

How often do we all do it during our day, when someone isn't quick enough, doesn't do things the way they should be done, etc.? We all do it. Why?

With so little effort, we can choose not to engage and allow them to do what they are doing without getting negatively emotionally involved.

We can, instead, choose inner peace.

Sheep only need a single flock, but people need two: one to belong to and make them feel comfortable, and another to blame all of society's problems on.

James Rozoff

March 2

Choices

I wake up every morning at nine, and grab the for the morning paper. Then, I look at the obituary page. If my name is not on it, I get up.

Benjamin Franklin

Are you having a good day or a bad day? Or come to that, just an indifferent day. Whichever it is, you are choosing to create it.

Our thoughts manifest themselves within us and within the people we are with.

If we look down on people, if we are critical or negative about them in any way, they respond in kind, at an unconscious level at the very least.

Whereas if we think loving, positive thoughts about them, they will reciprocate.

But what about when we are on our own? If we look out of the window when it is grey and dull and dwell on it, that's how we'll feel.

But if it is grey and dull, raining or freezing or far too hot for us, we can look out and feel the gratitude, joy, and excitement at being alive.

We can smile with the world, and it will smile back at us.

When you arise in the morning, think of what a precious privilege it is to be alive – to breathe, to think, to enjoy, to love.

Marcus Aurelius

Fear

The cave you fear to enter holds the treasure you seek.

Joseph Campbell

We create fear in our minds with our thoughts.

If we stop for a moment and consider our thoughts, we can appreciate how they create our feelings.

Whatever our feelings are, our thoughts are creating them.

And we know, although we may well fight against this idea, we know we can choose what we are thinking about.

Our ego and thoughts embellish the awfulness of what is to come, and we crash into all-consuming fear.

But what is to come (or isn't, more often than not) is different to where we are now. It will not be as we imagine it when we arrive there.

It will be a moment that we will go through. It will not be what we are projecting now.

We are creating our fears with our thoughts. If we change what we are thinking about now, the fear will disappear. The fear is not real. It is something we are choosing to create.

Don't choose to create something you don't want.

Choose to create something you want.

He who has overcome his fears will truly be free.

Aristotle

March 4

Loneliness

Loneliness is a sign that you are in desperate need of yourself.

Rupi Kaur

We can be surrounded by people but still be lonely.
We can be entirely alone and not be lonely.
There has to be a clue there somewhere.

Peace and contentedness lie within us. We know that, but we choose to forget it.

Seeing its chance, our ego showers us with ideas that may create instant gratification but do nothing to change our true inner feelings.

When was the last time you stopped everything and told yourself, 'I truly love you. I love you completely. You are amazing and wonderful. I am with you. We have power and energy. I love you. I love you. I love you.'

You need your own love to save your heart.

Rithvik Singh

March 5

Guilt

We each begin in innocence. We all become guilty.

Leonard F Peltier

Guilt's job is to draw your attention to something you've done, which is 'less than'. That's all.

Of course, we often take it as a cue to run the movies of shame and self-hatred so we can keep the total awfulness of the pain alive. Wallowing in it. But that is so self-indulgent.

Guilt points out what we've done, and then we have two choices.

The first is, 'Yes, it was bad, I'm not going to do it again'. And having made that decision, no more guilt.

The second choice is, 'It may be bad, but given who I am and the circumstances I'm in, I will continue to do it, for now anyway'. And once again, having made that decision, no more guilt.

Stop beating yourself up. It is not productive. It does not help. It makes you less than. Thank guilt for pointing it out, and get on with your life. Be positive.

If there is no intent, there's no guilt.

Titus Livius

March 6

Judgement

Hate your next-door neighbour, but don't forget to say grace.

P F Sloane

We may not do that.

But do we view others with love and tolerance?

Or do we judge?

Flashing out little mental spikes of disapproval, or even disgust.

Do we see people walking down the road, and with a quick piece of mental lightning, damn them for some extraordinary personal belief?

Do we shout abuse at other drivers when they misbehave? Whatever that means.

Would it not be nice to live in a state of peace, love and acceptance?

It is our choice.

Don't criticise what you can't understand.

Bob Dylan

March 7

Vegging

Doing nothing is very hard to do... you never know when you're finished.

Leslie Nielsen

Doing nothing is better than being busy doing nothing.

Lao Tzu

Sometimes, not often, my mind empties, and I want to sit and do nothing. Be a wilting vegetable.

I used to come out of it overwhelmed with guilt.

Now, I accept it with gentle gratitude. If that's how I feel, then it must be, at some level, what I need.

Have an indulgent bask in it.

It passes, and you come out of it ready to get on. It's okay.

Two percent of the people think, three percent of the people think they think, and ninety-five percent of the people would rather die than think.

George Bernard Shaw

Anger

Sometimes, when I get up in the morning, I feel very peculiar. I feel like I've just got to bite a cat! I feel like if I don't bite a cat before sundown, I'll go crazy! But then I take a deep breath and forget about it. That's what is known as real maturity.

Charles M Schulz – Snoopy

Do you ever feel angry?

If not, do you ever feel irritated?

Do things, as they say, get up your nose?

The cause of anger is fear.

You may well react (angrily?) to that and say – 'Well, mine isn't based on fear!'

But bear with me for a moment. Peel away the layers below your anger. Now peel away some more layers. If/when you go deep enough, you will find fear.

And then consider if anger is the best, the most sensible way to cope with your fear.

I'm yet to find any instance when it was. Anger disempowers me. It is not a good way to achieve the outcome I want. Ever.

So, I discard it and choose some other way of behaving.

But that's just me. You may be special and different?

There is no illusion greater than fear.

Lao Tzu

If you are pained by external things, it is not they that disturb you, but your own judgement of them. And it is in your power to wipe out that judgement now.

Marcus Aurelius

March 9

Trust

Making the hard decision to throw away a once favourite bra is like deleting an ex-friend that repeatedly let you down.

Crystal Woods

If we work with someone or have a relationship with someone who frequently fails to do what they say they will, it becomes very difficult to trust them. We are constantly on the lookout for yet another disappointment.

And are we guilty of this? Do we say to ourselves that we will do or won't do something and then fail to carry it through?

Every time we do that, it punctures our self-belief. It wounds us. We like ourselves just a little bit less.

It is good to think carefully before we say we will or won't do something and then choose whether to go ahead with it. Each time we commit and achieve, we have success, and we like and trust ourselves more. It is easier to love ourselves.

Doing what needs to be done may not make you happy, but it will make you great.

George Bernard Shaw

Blame

What can everyone do? Praise and blame. This is human virtue, this is human madness.

Friedrich Nietzsche

How easy it is to jump into blaming others without ever (or seldom) glancing at our shortcomings.

And it is so easy to do it in totally different areas of our lives as we allow the flames of resentment to dance in us.

And who suffers?

We do.

So why choose to suffer?

Let it go.

Just let it go and get on with living your own life.

If someone is always to blame, if every time something goes wrong, someone has to be punished, people quickly stop taking risks. Without risks, there can't be breakthroughs.

Peter Diamandis

Struggle

The most beautiful people we have known are those who have known defeat, known suffering, known struggle, known loss and have found their way out of the depths.

Elisabeth Kubler-Ross

Struggle is the norm. We have life. We have struggles. Some are big, but most of them are small.

The more we battle with them, the more harm they do to us.

Someone at home, at work, in the supermarket does something that 'irritates' us. You can make the word 'irritates' bigger or smaller. So it happens, and we react. And then... well then it is up to us, isn't it?

But here's a thought. If life is littered with struggles, why not just accept that, say, 'Next' and get on with our day?

And as we do that, we can remember all the struggles we have been through that give us our strength today. So greet the struggles with delight, knowing you are growing and becoming more because of them.

Turn your wounds into wisdom.

Oprah Winfrey

Rules

Do not seek to rule any man other than yourself.

Lailah Gifty Akita

The hell with the rules. If it sounds right, then it is.

Eddie Van Halen

Because I do not do something, it does not mean that other people should not do it. And likewise, just because you do something doesn't mean it's wrong if they don't.

The trouble is that we have rules for ourselves and often apply those rules to others. And when they do not behave in the way that conforms with 'our rules', it causes us distress.

Some people have rules for themselves but not for others. This is very liberating. If you sit down to eat a meal with someone who starts their meal with a large bowl of ice cream rather than the main course, you can discard all the stress it causes you. You can wonder if that might be a better way to eat a meal.

If you have rules for yourself and others, experiment with discarding your rules for them. It may be enlightening. You may learn something. You will undoubtedly feel less stressed.

You are remembered for the rules you break.

Douglas MacArthur

Isolation

The worst thing someone gets is isolated. Isolation is the darkest part of any condition.

Annie Lennox

Often, when we are unhappy (unhappy covers an immeasurable array of negative emotions), we withdraw. We creep under the duvet and hide. We isolate. Isolation never leads to a solution. It just intensifies it.

Talking and listening with others will enable us to work towards a solution.

Discontent, blaming, complaining, self-pity cannot serve as a foundation for a good future, no matter how much effort you make.

Eckhart Tolle

March 14

Pain

Every failure is a gift. Every pain is an opportunity.

Maxime Lagacé

Oh, how we cling to pain, finding ways to keep it alive.
You cry, 'Hey, I don't do that!'

If that's true, you are the exception because most of us do things to keep the pain alive that little bit longer. We take it with us and discuss it with others, becoming obsessed with it. We wallow.

And pain cannot be avoided. We all suffer pain, and it is one of the things that gives light and dimension to joy. Pain gives us wisdom and understanding.

All our lives, we've been on a roller coaster with times of intense pain, and yet here we are. We have survived. We will again. The sooner we let go and move on from our current pain, with the certain knowledge that it will pass, the better.

Be patient and tough; someday, this pain will be useful to you.

Ovid

Love

Have enough courage to trust love one more time and always one more time.

Maya Angelou

Feel love. Feel it throughout your body. Fill your body and your mind with love. Bathe in it.

Do not just read those words.

Really stop and completely embrace love. Be embraced by love.

It feels different to how you felt before or how you usually feel. It feels like total love, with no expectation of something in return. It is just becoming love.

Take your time. Enjoy.

Now, think of someone you barely know or don't know. The checkout person at the supermarket. Encompass them with your love.

Now think of someone who has annoyed you recently or who does irritate you and envelope them in your love.

So here's the challenge for today or forever – go through your days, giving/feeling love wherever you go, whatever you do, to as many people as possible. (When you forget and stop doing it, remember and start again.)

See how the world, your day, and you are changed.

Delight in it.

Where there is love, there is life.

Mahatma Gandhi

March 16

Anger

Freedom is the only worthy goal in life. It's won by disregarding things that lie beyond our control.

Epictetus

A person capable of angering you becomes your master.

Epictetus

Anger is not just anger.

And when we lose our temper, we can fall into the trap of believing, 'it is who we are.'

Or we do things and find ourselves saying, 'That wasn't like me.'

Our judgement is affected. Our thought process altered.

Then, after anger, after we have resolved or accepted it, it turns into sadness.

That sadness that fills us drains us and disempowers us.

And we are still allowing 'them' to be our master.

We want to learn to step away and discard our unwanted emotions.

We want to be our masters, leading ourselves in our chosen direction. No longer jerked around by others.

Meditation, stillness, calm. Rational conversation. Self-belief. These are all things that can help to create peace of mind.

You always seek to control others when you are not in full ownership of yourself.

Cicely Tyson

If you can't control peanut butter, you can't expect to control your life.

Bruce Colville

Service

One of the secrets of life is that all that is really worth doing is what we do for others.

Lewis Carroll

Think about that for a moment.

All that is worth doing is what we do for others. And yet... how often is that the case? So much of our time is spent on self-obsession, satisfying ourselves, and looking for ways to make our lives just a little bit better.

At the end of the day, we have failed. It is still the same old, same old.

We go to bed without being satisfied, our new toy abandoned or just incorporated into our life with no real continued joy.

To which you may shout, 'Hey! Hey! What are you saying? That may apply to you... but leave me out of that... I'm okay... I'm doing okay.'

'Well, well done, I'm glad to hear that, but is that the honest truth?'

And looking at the quote again, if that is true, and I suspect it is, how many gold stars have you accumulated today?

Who did you <u>completely</u> listen to or help?

Many of you spend your life doing amazing things, looking after people in one way or another. Have a basket load of gold stars.

Just one question, though, did you stop doing this when you got home to your family?

I know I could do far more. I'm working on it. I know I will never do as much as I think I could.

Unless someone like you cares a whole awful lot, nothing is going to get better. It's not.

Dr Seuss

Spiders

Incy Wincy spider
Climbed up the waterspout
Down came the rain
And washed the spider out.

Nursery Rhyme

My grandmother, bless her, always had a towel hanging in the bath.

'Why, Granny?' I asked when I was six. I may not have been six. I may never have asked, who can remember?

'It's so the spiders can escape. They can't climb up the sides of the bath. Of course, people think they've crawled up out of the plughole, but they haven't.'

And so I always have a towel hanging in my bath. Pity the poor spiders.

My mother early on taught us to respect all animals, and I mean all animals – not just cats and dogs but rats and snakes and spiders and fish and wildlife, so I really grew up believing they are just like us and just as deserving of consideration.

Joanna Lumley

Nothingness

Nothing is mine, not even body, not even thoughts. This realisation is the door to absolute freedom and supreme power.

Shunya

If you count to ten, you go one, two, three etc. All the known things.

But stop for a moment and consider zero. Zero is the unknown thing that comes before one. Zero is nothingness.

Back-peddle with me. Come into zero. Come into the nothingness that exists before any of the known things.

Empty your mind for a moment and allow yourself to fall into zero. Into nothingness. Into the entity that is there.

Can nothing be an entity?

There is undoubtedly a clarity of mind there. An uncluttered peace. A launch pad to take you into gentle knowing. A place that we know we will benefit from every time we go there.

Love and peace.

Everything that's created comes out of silence. Your thoughts emerge from the nothingness of silence. Your words come out of this void. Your very essence emerged from emptiness. All creativity requires some stillness.

Wayne Dyer

March 20

Action

*You cannot escape the responsibility of tomorrow by
evading it today.*

Abraham Lincoln

Forgive me for asking.
Forgive me for intruding
But...
What have you been putting off?
Today is the day.
Today is the day to do it. Or, at the very least, start to do
it.
Make a firm plan for its continuation and completion.
You are hurting yourself by not doing it. Do it.
Do it today.

Someday is not a day of the week.

Janet Dailey

He who has begun has half done. Dare to be wise; begin.

Horace

Adventure

To be alive at all involves some risk.

Harold Macmillan

We think we are alive. We believe we are important, achieving and participating.

But are we really? Or are we simply pouring out the same tired old rubbish our parents did?

Do we dare to take risks?

Do we allow ourselves to have adventures?

Do we meditate deeply?

Do we discuss our decisions with the still, quiet voice within? Or does our noisy ego push us into the world and its chosen existence?

So many questions.

Have you discovered a simple answer?

Have you ever looked?

If you dare nothing, then when the day is over, nothing is all you will have gained.

Neil Gaiman

March 22

Action

Yada Yada Yada
Let's stop talking talking talking
Taking up our lives
Saying things that don't make sense
Hoping help arrives

Dory Previn

So much of so many conversations are just a waste of time. Simply making noises to fill the space and convince ourselves that we will do... It's so much better to say nothing until you are ready to be honest.

Honest!

Well, well, that's an idea.

[If I don't tell you and you don't tell me, then it doesn't exist, and we can go about our meaningless day. Pretending.]

To change takes courage.

Where will it lead?

If it leads you somewhere now rather than in three or seven years, then that's undoubtedly better.

Don't waste years hoping things will change.

Change them now and live.

Burying your head in the sand does not make you invisible,
it only leads to suffocation.

Wayne Gerard Trotman

March 23

Gossip

Whoever gossips to you will gossip about you.

Spanish Proverb

Even if we do not consider ourselves gossips, we almost certainly talk about others. It is human. And we care about them.

We do want to be mindful of it, though. It is so easy to say or repeat things that should go no further.

If you must slander someone, don't speak it – but write it – write it in the sand, near the water's edge.

Napoleon Hill.

Moving On

There is only one difference between slaughter and laughter and that's an S. It's all two sides of one thing and you got to make sure you're on the laughing side.

Ana Salote

A couple of months ago, a friend moved into a new house with her family. New house gives the wrong impression really. It was an old house that needed a vast amount of work doing to it, while they lived in it. New roof, staircase, front door, toilets, kitchen, etc., to give you an idea of the potential mayhem.

It turned out that her builder was totally useless and a liar. She finally sacked him and discovered that most of the things he'd done needed re-doing.

One's immediate reaction to hearing about his lunacy is to say, 'Sue him'. But my second and wiser reaction is don't sue him.

I've met a handful of people over the years who have sued people for varying amounts of money, and the anger they experienced was unbelievable. It's certainly not worth the money, even if they got it in the end.

So let it go. Thank God for your learning experience. Get on with your life, and be grateful for the blessings.

Don't feed your resentment bucket.

Live today.

Enjoy.

There is a big difference between giving up and knowing when you've had enough.

Joanne Reed

A man's only got so many yeses inside him before he uses them all up.

Pat Conroy

Parents

It is amazing how people can change behind closed doors.

Susan Kessen

Wounded parents often inflict pain and suffering on their children.

David W Earle

This is not a cautionary tale. A cautionary thought perhaps, and sadly, it comes far too late for many people.

Before you marry or commit to a long-term relationship, spend a weekend with your potential partner's parents.

And at the end of that time, ask yourself. Do I want to spend the next 20-40 years living with these people? Because, in all likelihood, that is what you're committing to. You are going to marry a junior version of them.

Now, some people have amazing, wonderful parents, and if you find them, hold on tight.

It has been my observation that parents kill more dreams than anybody.

Spike Lee

Being

If you are brave enough to say goodbye, life will reward you with a new hello.

Paulo Coelho

We are not the person we present to the world. We are a fiction of our creation.

Within our heart, there is peace and wholeness. That is us.

Go into your heart and allow yourself to be the miracle you truly are.

Take time.

Delve.

Discover.

Be.

Live the beautiful, authentic truth inside your heart.

Amy Leigh Mercree

What you feel is what you feel. Just because someone else doesn't have the same experience or it sounds weird, doesn't mean it's not true.

Natalie K Martin

Unconscious

Procrastination is opportunity's assassin.

Victor Kiam

Our unconscious listens to everything we say and does its best to make that our reality.

So, for example, if we say or think, 'I'm no good at that.' Our unconscious will do its best to make that the truth.

I do not know if you pray or have positive affirmations that you use, but when people do, many tend to rush through the words quickly and without thought. Saying the words so quickly, they become meaningless.

It is far, far better to choose just a couple of important things and say them slowly with feeling, emotion and belief.

Say them so you can feel them in your body.

Do that, and notice the change.

Be not afraid of growing slowly, be afraid only of standing still.

Chinese Proverb

Gratitude

It is only with gratitude that life becomes rich.

Dietrich Bonhoeffer

Gratitude unlocks the fullness of life.

Melody Beattie

How do you start your day? What are your thoughts as you awake? Love and gratitude?

What are the first words out of your mouth? How do you greet the first person you interact with? What do you say or think about the first thing you eat or drink?

Does any of that make a difference?

Yes, a massive one. It sets your whole day on a stronger track as the day progresses.

Love and gratitude.

Enrich your life.

You are the one who makes a difference to it. Choose wisely.

The single greatest thing you can do to change your life today would be to start being grateful for what you have right now. And the more grateful you are, the more you get.

Oprah Winfrey

Lessons

The old saying is that when life gives you lemons, make lemonade. I say f**k that. I say when life gives you lemons, make margaritas.

Kristin Neff

Certainly, after a few of them, you'll forget the lemons!

But no matter what life throws at you, you have a choice about how you view it.

Even in the blackest moment, there is still life. There are people who are important to you and to whom you are important.

Our lives and the events in them are intwined, we need both the good, the bad and even the impossible to make the whole.

Hang in there. Let the impossible run its course. It will. It will become a memory. It will be replaced.

Breathe. Breathe again. Focus only on your breath. It will change. Be patient. We've been there. We know.

When life gives you lemons, learn to juggle.

James Patterson

A grapefruit is just a lemon that saw an opportunity and took advantage of it.

Oscar Wilde

Happiness

Nothing can bring you happiness but yourself.

Ralph Waldo Emerson

Some people are so much happier than others. And that being the case, it must be possible for us to be happier. (Unless we are already one of the truly happy ones.)

If we study people who are happy, calm, and serene, we will realise that one of the main reasons they can achieve this is because they focus on the positive.

They do not complain about others and are happy to take them as they are. They do not consume all the negative news that pours from the TV.

Yes, they keep up with what they need to know for work, but that is all. They do not indulge in hours of soap operas. They watch uplifting things.

They don't spend their lives judging people, trying to correct or control them. They look for ways to bring light, love and laughter into the world.

If you want to be happy, be.

Leo Tolstoy

The only person you are destined to become is the person you decide to be.

Ralph Waldo Emerson

Living

One can choose to go back toward safety or forward toward growth. Growth must be chosen again and again; fear must be overcome again and again.

Abraham Maslow

It is so easy to stick our heels in and say no. Even if we are usually quite adventurous, most people's default setting when they are offered a new way to do something is to hesitate or say 'No' immediately.

Of course, our years of experience have taught us how to do things the 'right' way, so that's what is most comfortable for us. And I am not suggesting that you are wrong. I'm just suggesting that there might be mileage in considering new alternatives.

In fact, I think experimenting with alternatives keeps us alive. Puts zing into our day. It keeps us young. Brings laughter and fun into our day.

Life begins at the end of your comfort zone.

Neale Donald Walsch

If not

you...

who?

Living

It's the children the world almost breaks who grow up to save it.

Frank Warren

The more we suffer, the more we have suffered, the greater our potential for strength, growth and the ability to actually do something with our lives.

Those who have an easy, comfortable life just go on without making any waves. Just accepting things as they are.

So, if we are having a hard time, we do not want to feel bad about it.

Instead be grateful that something worthwhile is likely to come out of it.

Have courage. Keep going. Enjoy the journey.

So early in my life, I had learned that if you want something, you had better make some noise.

Malcolm X

To live is to suffer, to survive is to find meaning in the suffering.

Gordon Allport

April 2

Mistakes

When you get exhausted, frustrated, overwhelmed, or run down, your body is saying that you are doing things that are none of your business. God does not require of you what is beyond your ability, what leads you away from God, or what makes you depressed or sad.

Henri J M Nouwen

We try so hard.

We try, and we fail. Yet again. And we hate ourselves a little bit more. We don't even have the energy required to spiral down the plug hole. We just lean over and belly-flop into the morass below.

And when we feel like that, we dredge up all the inadequacy we have accumulated since birth.

We were told what we should not do from the moment we were born. We might have been told how good we were if we were lucky. But we remember that less well because it was not accompanied with the pain of criticism.

So here we are now, with our enormous trunk filled with blame, failure and criticism. And it seizes any opportunity it has to slash you with the pain again.

Realise that the things you did were what you needed to do to learn how to live in this world.

Thank yourself for the courage and strength that has got you this far.

Allow yourself to learn how to live.

Allow yourself to make mistakes.

Your pain is deep, and it won't just go away. It is also uniquely yours, because it is linked to some of your earliest life experiences.

Henri J M Nouwen

The way we talk to our children becomes their inner voice.

Peggy O'Mara

Living

The chief enemy of creativity is good sense.

Pablo Picasso

Be creative.
Be spontaneous.
Do creative things.
Do things differently. Stretch and challenge yourself. Embrace being alive.
Every time we do anything which awakens our brain, every part of our being benefits.
Most people are like an abandoned piece of old machinery, left, long forgotten, in the corner of the shed.
Get it out. Oil it. Love it. Bring it back to life.
Let it live.

We have to continually be jumping off cliffs and developing our wings on the way down.

Kurt Vonnegut

Punctuality

Better three hours too soon than a minute too late.

William Shakespeare – The Many Wives of Windsor

My inbuilt behaviour with appointments is to get there slightly early. In my teens and early twenties, I would arrange to meet friends in a pub, the cinema, or in the street.

One day, standing in the rain waiting for friends, I looked at my watch, and they were fifteen minutes late. 'Right, that's it. I will never wait more than fifteen minutes for anyone ever again.' And I left.

And by and large, I have kept to that throughout my life. I have occasionally warned people not to be more than fifteen minutes late.

This was, of course, long before mobile phones. In fact, in 1970, only 30% of houses had phones.

I only wrote this because the other day, I went to the chiropractor and waited forty-five minutes before leaving, in pain, vowing to find a new chiropractor.

My time, my life, is too valuable to spend it waiting for people.

Tomorrow is nothing, today is too late, the good lived yesterday.

Marcus Aurelius

A man doesn't know what happiness is until he gets married. By then, it's too late.

Frank Sinatra

April 5

Self-Care

Self-care is not selfish. You cannot serve from an empty vessel.

Eleanor Brown

It is so easy not to take proper care of oneself.

I won't suggest ways you might do this, I don't want to put ideas into your head. But everything you put into your body, through your mouth, your eyes, and your ears, impacts your being at a core level.

Why not take a little time today to consider whether there are things that it would be wise not to consume?

I don't need three cars, a great big fucking house (for two people). But I do and I want it. This is the issue.

Geoffrey West

Change

How wonderful it is that nobody need wait a single moment before starting to improve the world.

Anne Frank

Hey, that must mean that it is something that I can do.

If I can start improving the world without you or them, then there must be something that I can do within me because you and they are not always here.

But what can I do?

Hang on, I've got it.

It is how I choose to think and how I view and interact with the world.

It must be whether I am choosing to be right or choosing to have peace.

Every single person has the power to change the world and help people.

Laura Marano

Inner Voice

*You are your master. Only you have the master keys to
open the inner locks.*

Amit Ray

Our inner voice, the voice of love and peace, is always there. All the time. Always.

All we have to do is choose to access and listen to it. To ask for it to guide the way we think.

We simply have to ask and listen.

It will cut through and silence all the insane screaming of our ego. It will quietly let us know what is the right thing to say, do or think.

It is love and peace.

The more we use it, the stronger it gets until it becomes our dominant thought process.

The ego will still be there, making its demands, but we will find it easier to ignore them.

*At the core of your heart, you are perfect and pure. No one
and nothing can alter that.*

Amit Ray

April 8

Peace

Do not let the behaviour of others destroy your inner peace.

Dalai Lama

There have been times for me, when the very idea of peace of mind, had as much chance of existing as an invisible speck of dust on the far side of a vast room. I knew that it existed, it must, but the chances of ever finding it again... (and that was before I got my puppy.)

Seriously though, there are times when the whole world seems to have collectively decided to do me in.

And the sad thing (if I have enough humility to acknowledge it) is that none of it has anything to do with the f'ing world. It's all down to me.

If I want peace of mind, all I have to do is look within and claim it. (Fat chance of that when I'm ranting.)

It is always there, waiting patiently for me to embrace it.

Love. Love for myself. Love for the world. So full of peace. Sounds really appealing.

Those who tried to break you are expecting you to be in fight mode. Conquer them with your peace.

Thema Davis

Everybody has a plan until they get punched in the mouth.

Mike Tyson

Life

It is what it is, it is what you make it.

James Durbin

'Is this all there is?'

Do you ever have a thought, a question like that, that slides across your mind?

Or, for that matter, if you do not have that question, is it one you would do well to ask?

Clearly, there is more than this.

There are several billion alternatives.

Do we actually want any of them?

Most of them we certainly do not want.

But if you are not satisfied with the 'all this' that you have, then it can change. All you have to do is change how you process things and what you currently do.

However locked into your life you are, even if you cannot change anything else, you can alter your attitude toward it.

Very little is needed to make a happy life; it is all within yourself, in your way of thinking.

Marcus Aurelius

April 10

Saving

Death destroys a man, but the idea of death saves him.

E M Forster

I was on a budget plane, and the stewardess made the preflight announcements. She was not sticking to her script and was very funny. For once, everyone was listening to her.

'If the oxygen masks drop down and you are with your children, put your own mask on first. If you have two children, decide which one you love the most.'

And it is an interesting question if you ponder it for a moment. Who in your life, adult or child, would you save first?

If all the people in your life were drowning, who would you save first?

And then, if you were allowed one more, who would that be? (Don't worry, you don't have to tell anyone your answers.)

Who do you spend the most time with?

because sometimes the people we need to save us, are really the people that need saving themselves.

r m drake

To save a man's life against his will is the same as killing him.

Horace

April 11

Joy

There may be peace without joy, and joy without peace, but the two combined make happiness.

John Buchan

Joy and peace are natural. So why do we spend so much of our lives not experiencing them?

Why do we indulge in disquiet, anger, fear and, most often, just nothingness? Hauling ourselves through another day, towards the night, waiting until we can switch it all off for a few hours.

Maybe that is not how you view your day. But is it really as good as it could be? Is it not cluttered with the mundane and the yet again?

And yet joy and peace are natural. So why are we not living drenched in them?

It is our ego, enticing us into the thrill and pain of negativity. Of judging and belittling ourselves and others.

We have another voice, the inner voice of love and peace, we can go into and claim our peace whenever we want to.

Peace and joy are the basic requirements for a life of well-being.

Sadhgura

April 12

Living

Smartphone is definitely smarter than us to be able to keep us addicted to it.

Munia Khan

When I was young, not every house had a phone. Those that did tended to have it in the hallway (which was cold, and everyone could listen to your conversation).

Sometime later, answering machines appeared.

But we left our houses and got on with our day and our lives without a phone. We managed!

No, managed is quite the wrong word – we lived. We were alive. We interacted with others and the world. We looked around us, breathed in the scents, and listened to the noises. We were there.

So here is an idea. Leave your phone at home. The world will not end. In fact, it will begin.

Liberate yourself from its stifling grasp. If you do take it with you, switch it off until you genuinely <u>have</u> to use it.

Train your brain to find new connections, innovations, opportunities and possibilities that otherwise would have been missed.

Maria Forleo

April 13

Advice

I always pass on good advice. It is the only thing to do with it. It is never of any use to oneself.

Oscar Wilde

They say that everyone we meet is here to teach us something.

If that is true about my brother-in-law, God help the world.

I was wallpapering the front room, and he came and stood in the doorway.

I should mention that he has no volume control on his voice, he broke it, and it's stuck on very loud. So there he is in the doorway, me halfway up a ladder. He proceeded to shout at me for fifteen minutes, telling me how it should be done and why it shouldn't be done the way that I was doing it.

(I didn't stand on the ladder for the fifteen minutes, I got on with the wallpapering.)

The only good thing was that he did not offer to help or demonstrate how it should be done.

After fifteen minutes, I guess he had said everything that needed saying (sorry, needed shouting), and he charged off into the kitchen to explain something to his sister. Probably how to boil the kettle...

Teacher...? Well, not about wallpapering.

But... perhaps about tolerance. Maybe it is about choosing when to spend time with him. (Never sounds a bit too often.) Still, you've got to be grateful you're alive, haven't you?

Never miss a good chance to shut up.

Will Rogers

Compliments

I can live for two months on a good compliment.

Mark Twain

Oh, how we love compliments, even if we think we don't mind about them. We do.

We feel good if we spend time with people in our new gear or with a new hairdo, and some of them compliment us. Special but not overwhelmed – after all, compliments don't really matter to us, do they? We are above that kind of thing.

A while later, we wear the same clothes, hair, whatever, and no one compliments us. We feel slightly let down.

Then we go out for the third time, and no one even notices us. And we think, 'I need to get some new clothes or a new hairstyle.'

And so we do.

We have to keep our ego fed, don't we?

There is nothing you can say in answer to a compliment. I have been complimented myself a great many times, and they always embarrass me... I always feel that they have not said enough.

Mark Twain

April 15

Action

No one is useless in this world who lightens the burdens of another.

Charles Dickens

If you want to be happy and fulfilled, do something for someone else without the expectation of getting anything in return.

Except you will get something in return. You'll get the joy and the uplift that comes from having done it.

You and they will both have benefitted. The world will have benefitted.

So do things for others. Spread the wellness throughout the world.

And when others want to do things for you, accept it with grace and gratitude.

When we give cheerfully and accept gratefully, everyone is blessed.

Maya Angelou

Overwhelm

*The vastness of my now-unending existence yawned open
before me. I let it swallow me whole.*

Sarah J Maas

Sometimes, we are overwhelmed by thoughts. An endless bombardment, one following the last, faster than we can blink, nearly all filled with one kind of poison or another. Endless. Draining.

Stop.

Look at one of them.

Just concentrate only on one thought. Ask yourself what you can do about it right now? If there is anything, do it.

Most of the time, there is nothing we can do now. Travel forward in your mind, honestly, and see what you can do and when you can do it. Be specific. Agree with yourself to 'do it then.'

Thank the thought and then discard it until its appointed time. If it reappears, tell it to go away. You've made a contract with it. It does not need to reappear before then.

Next, ask if any other thoughts need to be considered.

If you feel overwhelmed, take on another project.

Roy Halston Frowick

Seriously

Seriousness is a disease.

Rajneesh

The opposite of play is not work. It's depression.

Brian Sutton-Smith

We pull our grown-up clothes tightly around us and march, yes march, off to do our duty. (Job.)

Please do not bother me now! I am thinking! I am important! (Even if I'm not sure I'm important, I have to pretend that I am, or everyone will crucify me.) Where's the fun in that?

And we wonder why there is so much anger and madness in the world.

I am sitting at my desk, and the kingfisher just flew by. Did you know that the blue feathers on its back are, in fact, brown? The bright blue colour that we see is due to a phenomenon called structural colouration.

Lighten up y'all.

I still get wildly enthusiastic about the little things... I play with leaves. I skip down the street and run against the wind.

Leo Buscaglia

Grown up, and that is a terribly hard thing to do. It is much easier to skip it and go from one childhood to another.

F Scott Fitzgerald

Doing Good

I believe that every human mind feels pleasure in doing good to another.

Thomas Jefferson

Do you do good? Now that's a question. We want to answer, 'Yes, of course, I do,' but the little voice comes in and says, 'Are you sure?' Followed by 'When was the last time?' And then, 'Well, certainly not all the time.'

And so we settle on, 'Well, I have good intentions. I don't go out of my way to do bad. No, hang on, that didn't come out how I meant it to.' I meant, 'I want to do good, and I think and hope that I do good most of the time.'

'Hell – what kind of question is that anyway?'

Doing good may not have to be overt. Perhaps just being there is enough. Doing good feels good for you and the others involved. Doing good is a gentle, honest openness. No judgement, just love.

And it flows out from us and back to us, showering us with its petals as it goes.

To be doing good deeds is man's most glorious task.

Sophocles

Living

To love at all is to be vulnerable. Love anything, and your heart will certainly be wrung and possibly broken. If you want to make sure of keeping it intact, you must give your heart to no one, not even an animal. Wrap it carefully round with hobbies and little luxuries; avoid all entanglements; lock it up safe in the casket or coffin of your selfishness. But in that casket – safe, dark, motionless, airless – it will change. It will not be broken; it will become unbreakable, impenetrable, irredeemable.

C S Lewis

Go out.
Take risks.
Live.
The pain is worth it.
Be open.
Experience life.
Live.

Don't you ever get the feeling that all your life is going by and you're not taking advantage of it? Do you realise you've lived nearly half of the time you have to live already?

Ernest Hemingway

Live life to the fullest, for the future is scarce.

Nick Carter

Staying Alive

It's not so important staying alive, it's staying human that's important. What counts is that we don't betray each other.

George Orwell

We are not tied to the person we were twenty years ago, last year, or even yesterday. We can change. We have changed. We are constantly changing. But many of those changes happened without our even noticing or any conscious input.

It is so comfortable to be stuck in our ways. To repeat, repeat, repeat, without thought.

The question we might want to consider is, 'Do we want to be stuck in a rut?'

Or do we want to march forward alive and open to new ways of interacting with others and ourselves?

Love is how you stay alive even after you are gone.

Mitch Albom

Growth

*What the caterpillar calls the end of the world, the master
calls a butterfly.*

Richard Bach

I remember walking up a black metal staircase to someone's house and seeing that the top few steps were covered in rice. I went on a little and realised that the rice was moving. The rice was maggots. I turned and left. Never to return.

Since then, I have always thought of maggots as reincarnated rice. It helps.

Whether we are, at a given moment in our lives, a caterpillar or a reincarnated rice, one thing is for sure. We will change.

The fact is that we have been doing this all our life. Struggling through some difficulty, huge or small, to arrive stronger on the other side of it.

And it helps to realise, as we go through our current difficulty or the next one, that we will come out of it stronger and better able to deal with the next thing life so generously gives us.

*I don't really understand that process called reincarnation,
but if there is such a thing, I'd like to come back as my
daughter's dog.*

Leonard Cohen

April 22

Memories

*All you have to do is realise that the past is now only a
ghostly memory kept alive by digging into the archives of
your stagnated memories,*

Sydney Banks

The truth is if we dare to prise that rock up out of the
mud and bend our face down so that we can see its belly, the
truth is that we like to keep the pain alive.

No, that's not true. Our ego likes to keep it alive. Our ego
relishes in the destructive power that those memories have
over us. 'God forbid', the ego cries, 'that we might ever
escape.'

But the memories do not possess you. They only have
power over you if you let them.

Acknowledge them, then slide them back under the stone
where they belong. They do not need to puncture you or your
soul.

And, although this may come as a surprise to you, you do
not live in the past. You live now. In this moment. Here now.

Reject the ghostly memories. They have no power in the
present unless you give them space.

When you let go of them, you feel the freedom of being
alive.

*We experience less pain in reality than we do in our
imaginations.*

Atef Ashab Uddin Sahil

Suffering

Man cannot remake himself without suffering, for he is both the marble and the sculptor.

Alexis Carrel

Life is full of misery, loneliness and suffering – and it's all over much too soon.

Woody Allen

Is your ego holding you hostage? Is it in charge? Is it making you judgemental, controlling, pathetic, subservient, hostile or false?

Is it preventing you from being real, the inner you, the light shining you? So many of us go along with the negative bullshit the ego inflicts on us because it requires no effort. We sink into a feather mattress of negativity.

Moving into positivity, our inner self, and an outlook of love requires no effort. The challenge is, or can be, moving from negativity to love and peace.

It's a question of, 'How much do I want to suffer before I change?' We can suffer as much as we like. Suffering is always an option. It has wide open arms, longing to hug us.

Out of suffering have emerged the strongest souls; the most massive characters are seared with scars.

Kahlil Gibran

April 24

Pain

I see your pain and it's big, but I also see your courage, and it's bigger.

Glennon Doyle

Look into yourself. Look deeply and say to yourself, 'I see your pain, but I also see your courage.'

Repeat it. Aloud, if you like. Keep repeating it. With feeling. With understanding. With love.

'I see your pain.'

Let love flow into the hidden corners of your pain. Let love and strength flow throughout you with gratitude.

'I see your courage.'

All things pass. In the future, as in the past, there will be times of greater and smaller difficulty and of greater and smaller happiness.

I see your pain, but I also see your courage.

You are not alone. You are never alone.

Within you lies your strength, love and courage.

Embrace yourself.

You are alive.

Emotional pain cannot kill you, but running from it can. Allow. Embrace. Let yourself feel. Let yourself heal.

Vironika Tugaleva

April 25

Limbo

I am in limbo, and in limbo, there are no races, no prizes, no changes, no chances. There are merely degrees of endurance, and endurance was never my strong point.

Keri Hulme

There is a gap, a limbo, at the end of every event. It may be so fleeting that we don't notice it, simply moving straight on and into the next happening in our lives.

But sometimes, the end of the event is too big, a bereavement, a job loss, the end of a relationship, and we get stuck. We become unable to move on and into the life waiting for us.

All the things from the past keep draining us and dragging us back. And they taint everything with fear.

'Nothing will ever be the same.' 'I shall never get my security back.' 'All the joy has gone.' 'I'm never going to recover.'

It's very challenging. But staying in limbo with all the negatives is harder. And nobody wants us to suffer. We are doing that to ourself.

It is much better to recognise what is happening and choose to move on with and into action and security. It is hard, but it's better. We can return to being alive.

Have you ever wondered what language they speak in limbo?

Lee T Gallup

April 26

Routines

It's a hard thing to leave any deeply routine life, even if you hate it.

John Steinbeck

How often do you break your routine? Once a day, a week, a month, never?

Doing something different at the same time of the week isn't breaking your routine. It's part of your routine.

Yes, it may be head and shoulders above what many people do, but it is still just a routine.

When locked into a monotonous life, we start to wither and die.

Choose something now that will break your routine.

Please go on, do it.

Live.

Enjoy your life.

If one knocks oneself out of one's routine – and in so doing, knocks others gently out of theirs – then one can now and again create these momentary opportunities to be better than one is.

Kathleen Rooney

April 27

Disappointment

*Freddie experienced the sort of abysmal soul-sadness which
afflicts one of Tolstoy's Russian peasants when, after
putting in a heavy day's work, strangling his father,
beating his wife, and dropping the baby into the city
reservoir, he turns to the cupboards, only to find the vodka
bottle empty.*

P G Wodehouse

Disappointment.

A quiet and gentle poison.

It is so slight, so palatable, so expected as a way of life
that it nearly almost always goes unnoticed. It pokes its head
out of the earth like a worm, hoping for, but not expecting
rain, and then retreats, thinking, what's the point?

Others disappoint us.

We disappoint ourselves.

By and large, we only sometimes look at it. What's the
point? It isn't going to change anyway, so why bother?

But it makes sense to pull it out. To shine a light on it.
Discuss it with the offenders, be that yourself or others, and
agree to make changes if you can.

Even if, ultimately, the only change you make is one of
acceptance.

Otherwise, it'll gently grow, like the tiny pieces of straw
stacked on the camel's back.

Clear the air. You deserve clean air to breathe.

*He has the look of one who had drunk the cup of life and
found a dead beetle at the bottom.*

P G Wodehouse

Longed for him. Got him. Shit.

Margaret Atwood

Gratitude

When I started counting my blessings, my whole life turned around.

Willie Nelson

I write everything with a fountain pen. The writing flows out of me onto the page with beauty.

Sometimes, like today, when I'm writing, my dog thinks it would be a good idea to come and sit on my lap, which is both wonderful and challenging.

Isn't that amazing, isn't love amazing? Isn't the world fantastic, so full of magical things, so many things to be grateful for?

It is so uplifting to stop momentarily and feel gratitude for everything in our life and world.

I have even got a rainbow outside my window! A strong wind which is a challenge for most birds but an obvious delight for the seagulls.

So very much to be grateful for.

Think of the cup of tea or coffee, the food you've eaten for breakfast, and say a heartfelt, 'Thank you,' to all the people involved in getting it to your body.

There is so much, so very much to be grateful for.

Gratitude opens the door to the power, the wisdom, the creativity of the universe. You open the door through gratitude.

Deepak Chopra

Challenges

If you are busy focusing on falling bricks, you will never realise that they are truly stepping stones you need to cross over to the next phase of your life.

Kemi Sogunle

It is so easy when we are faced with challenges to do battle with them. To deny them. To attack everyone and anything involved with them. And in doing that, we give them more power.

The way to change them is to accept that they exist.

Stop and quietly look at what is happening. Look at the present moment. Accept the present moment, whatever it is.

Instead of thinking of it as an enemy. Work with it, not against it.

Change your perception.

Success is due to our stretching to the challenges of life. Failure comes when we shrink from them.

John C Maxwell

April 30

Relationships

The most painful thing is losing yourself in the process of loving someone too much and forgetting that you are special too.

Ernest Hemingway

You've got to learn to leave the table when love's no longer being served.

Nina Simone

Our relationships exist for the benefit of us all.

Relationships are not one-sided. They are not there so that one of you benefits while the other loses out.

Equality and respect are the foundation stones of any good relationship, and if you are in one that does not have this, then you want to question its value.

Of course, if you are the one who is taking advantage, then get out your knife and start cutting away at the ropes you have trapped the other person with. Become proud to be you.

If you are the prisoner, look seriously at the trap you are in, change it, or escape from it.

Equality and respect.

How could you possibly choose to exist in any other way?

Respect and equality.

We cannot love anybody with whom we cannot laugh.

Agnes Repplier

Surround yourself with only people who are going to lift you higher.

Oprah Winfrey

Keep

letting

go

Review

*As I review my life, I feel I must have missed the point,
either then or now.*

Mason Cooley

Are you a reviewer?

Do you write reviews for the things that you use, that fill your life with the meaning you want.

In only takes a few minutes and it makes such a difference to the world.

It's so wonderful for the person who created the product, service that you use.

It is so helpful to the people in the world that are thinking of buying it.

Make a commitment to write at least two reviews a year.

Review.

Be fulfilled.

Enjoy.

*A bad review is like baking a cake with all your best
ingredients and having someone sit on it.*

Danielle Steel

Isolation

The most terrible poverty is loneliness, and the feeling of being unloved.

Mother Teresa

Sometimes, I don't feel that I fit in with others. I feel that, in some way, I do not belong. That I am outside or isolated from you all. And generally, I hide this quite convincingly.

However, whenever I have let this secret out, people tell me that they feel like this as well.

And so it would seem that this 'feeling', however you label it, is universal.

Which seems extraordinary. And it somehow reduces the pain I may be inflicting on myself when I indulge in this kind of self-attack.

Maybe everyone in the whole damn world is scared of each other.

John Steinbeck.

Anxiety

*You don't have to control your thoughts. You just have to
stop letting them control you.*

Dan Millman

Anxiety, dis-ease, all-consuming worry that seems, at times, to permeate the whole of one's body and being. Enveloping us in uncontrollable coffee shakes.

Of course, most of the time, thank god, we are not in 'it.' We read those words with detachment. Unable, thank god again, to summon up the feelings that go with the anxiety and dis-ease.

But when we are in them. When we are there, the paranoia obscures any hope of ever escaping.

But if we take a moment and look closely at the anxiety and dis-ease, 99% of it is in the future. A future we can do nothing about until we reach it.

There are perhaps one or two things that we can do now, today, at this moment, and the rest is out of reach.

So, if we are clever enough and want to discard the pain of anxiety, we can focus on and do the one or two things. And when we are doing them, we can discard anxiety.

*What lies behind us and what lies before us are tiny matters
compared to what lies within us.*

Ralph Waldo Emerson

Hurt

Choose not to feel harmed – and you will not feel harmed.
Don't feel harmed – and you haven't been.

Marcus Aurelius

They cannot hurt you.

The only person who can do hurt to you – is you.

What happens is that when 'they' do something that is questionable, our ego grasps it, like a child high on birthday cake, screams, 'Wahey!' and plunges its oldest, sharpest, ugliest sword right into our most vulnerable and tender part. 'Come with me into the joy of misery!' It screams.

And we, like a lamb to the slaughter, trot along as quickly as we can to immerse ourselves in the pain.

But clearly, we do not need to do that. We can go into the inner peace and quiet within ourselves and allow the atrocities to float on past us.

And perhaps it is worth remembering that the bad and unpleasant things that happen are there so that we can grow. Every experience teaches us something, though we may not know what that is at the time.

The moment you accept what troubles you've been given,
the door will open.

Rumi

Judgement

What we see depends mainly on what we look for.

John Lubbock

I was talking to an alcoholic outside a supermarket who was asking for money. 'It's for alcohol,' he said. 'I'm not going to buy crack cocaine with it.'

Isn't it interesting how, when already in the gutter, it is still possible to look down on people?

And I cannot imagine that there are any of us who do not look down on others, even if only fleetingly.

We judge, and we think ourselves better.

With practice, we can do this less and less, which is important. Because when we condemn others, we condemn ourselves.

There is nothing more tragic in all the world than to know right and not do it.

Martin Luther King Jnr

You'll never find rainbows if you're looking down.

Charlie Chaplin

You can throw a seed away, but you can't stop it from growing into a tree.

Michael Bassey-Johnson

May 6

Possessions

A fish in the water that is thirsty needs serious professional counselling.

Kabir

It seems to me that so many of us suffer from thirst, even though we live with an abundance of water.

We constantly look for that 'thing' that will satisfy us. 'Just that'. Really, life without it is almost unbearable. 'Must have!' 'Must have!'

And then...

Well, you know the answer if you're honest. 'It' arrives, and within a short time, 'It' is laid aside, and we search for the next.

Oh, that we could only learn.

Even if only once.

That would make a difference.

Pick something that has a particular value to you and give it away.

Wayne Dyer

May 7

Half a life

To live a life half dead, a living death.

John Milton

Don't live half a life. Don't do things by halves.
Either do them or don't do them.
Don't prod your toe in the water. Either swim or go away.
It is fine to swim. It is fine to go away.
Have courage.
Don't hang with people you don't like.
Don't hide what you think and believe with half a lie.
It matters not whether they know the truth or not. What matters is that you know.
Speak or be silent. Either is fine.
Just don't waffle a load of half-truths.
It is better to be loved or hated than ignored.
Come on, jump in. The water is lovely.
And that is the truth.

He'd somehow lived a detached life, more like a spectator than a participant in his own existence.

Guillaume Russo

I have had a perfectly wonderful evening, but this wasn't it.

Groucho Marx

Focus

When one door closes, another opens; but we often look so long and so regretfully upon the closed door that we do not see the one that has opened for us.

Alexander Graham Bell

It is so easy to spend one's life looking at what was and the pain and emptiness that goes with that.

As long as our eyes are cast down, we cannot see the light ahead.

When you travel in a train, do you face forwards or backwards? They are very different experiences.

Resolve to search for the good and the thrill of the future.

You don't have to see the whole staircase, just take the first step.

Martin Luther King Jnr

Moving On

Every adversity, every failure, every heartache carries with it the seeds of an equal or greater opportunity.

Napoleon Hill

I am seventy-seven years old, and my life has had a mass of ups and downs. Downs into blackness and despair. And yet, as I have clawed my way out of the seemingly bottomless pit, I have always found something better to move towards. Something I would never have found if I had not been drowning.

The important part of the saying is the seed. Seeds are small and so easily overlooked. They want to be planted, nurtured and loved into growth. Then, they can illuminated in the sunshine.

When we are trapped in the blackness, it is so hard to believe and find the seed.

But it is there. Hunt. Live. Rejoice.

Worry never accomplishes anything. When you have a problem, it is best to concentrate on the solution to that problem, not the problem itself.

Thomas D Willhite

Your purpose is not something to be found, it is something to be created.

Itayi Garande

Complainers

*Complainers rule out happiness, mentioning it only as
something lost.*

Mason Cooley

Oh, the disaster mongers, the mega-negatives!! Who
spew the worlds awfulness over us if we let them.

I don't let them.

I had lunch with an old friend (someone I knew a long
time ago) the other day.

He launched into his views about what was wrong with
the world, and I just held my hand up and said, 'I don't want
to talk about that. Let's find something uplifting to talk
about. How is your son?'

(The news about his son wasn't good either – no surprise
there.)

But we managed to get through the hour without
mentioning covid or rape and murder.

Then we parted, both lying to each other about how we
should do this again soon.

I don't allow people to poison my mind with their
negative crap. I have too much self-respect for that.

*Any fool can criticise, condemn and complain – and most
fools do.*

Benjamin Franklin.

*The very fact that you are a complainer shows that you
deserve your lot.*

James Allen

Mistakes

The most important thing in life is not to capitalise on your successes – any fool can do that. The really important thing is to profit from your mistakes.

William Bolitho

Of course, that quote assumes that you are doing something.

Sadly, so many people go through their lives never really having success or daring to make a mistake.

They rattle along, waiting for the next thing to happen, always assuming that they are actually there when it does.

It is so important to have goals in one's life that one is moving towards, that require effort and input to achieve.

Unless we are actively moving toward something, we are simply plodding towards death.

If you're not prepared to be wrong, you'll never come up with anything original.

Ken Robins

Giving up is the only sure way to fail.

Gena Showalter

Pause

I love those who can smile in trouble, who can gather strength from distress, and grow brave by reflection.

Leonardo De Vinci

Sometimes – not often, probably – our brains get scrambled. A bit like eggs do or an uncooked cake that's been dropped on the floor.

And our thoughts seem to bump into each other rather than coming out crisp like.

It is probably a good idea to give ourselves a break, a rest when it happens, and let them settle down in their own time as bubbles do in a pan of water when you turn the flame off.

So now you know.

Which could be helpful if that ever happened in your life.

Relax, allow the mind to become empty and surprise yourself with the great treasure that begins to flower into your soul.

Paulo Coelho

Nagging

Don't count on the power of your love or your nagging to create something that wasn't there to begin with.

Harriet Lerner

Nagging sucks. We all know that. And anyway, it does not work.

But let's look at the bigger picture for a moment. Someone enters a room or their house, and the place is a mess. There are other people already there. The first person starts to tidy, put away, do.

And the others? Do they just sit and watch? Do they get up and participate?

Come to that, they have limbs and a brain, why could they not have done some of it themselves before the first person came in?

What are the feelings here? Disrespect? Anger? Selfishness? Superiority? Sloth? Why should...? Pathetic?

Have you ever been any of these people?

Is it time to change?

Truly smart people never complain.

Rudolfo Peon

I date this girl for two years, and then the nagging starts: 'I want to know your name...'

Mike Binder

Living

That breath that you just took... that's a gift.

Rob Bell

Life is a balance of holding on and letting go.

Rumi

It's a good day to be alive. Today. It's a good day. Whatever is happening, it is a good day to be alive.

It's a good day to take the next step.

We can only take one step at a time. All we can ever do is take the next step. We spend so much time worrying about or beating ourselves up because we are not doing the 5th, 9th or 13th step.

Stop. Let go. Do this step.

Do it as well as you can. The others will or won't arrive. Leave them alone until you reach them.

Enjoy this step. It is wonderful. It's a good day to be alive and taking it.

'We'll be friends forever, won't we Pooh?' Asked Piglet.

'Even longer.' Pooh answered.

A A Milne

Belittle

You cannot shame or belittle people into changing their behaviours.

Brene Brown

It is so easy to belittle our achievements and believe that we have not really changed or accomplished anything.

Yes, our ego, if pressed, might concede that we have done a little but not much. We haven't changed. And if we have, it's just a pretence that we are fooling ourselves and the world with. Deep down, where the truth lies, the ego assures us that we are still a failure, still less than, just a phoney.

And all the while, our quiet inner voice waits patiently for its invitation to embrace us with a gentle smile. With calm inner peace, with love. Enabling us to go out and achieve even more.

Our ego looks on, jumping up and down on the sidelines, waiting for a chance to dash out and drag us down again. It knows the chance will come. It knows we are only human.

A friend is the wax that keeps the flame lit, an enemy is the wind that blows it out.

Anthony Liccione

May 16

Names

How vain, without merit, is the name.

Homer

The moment we give anything or anyone a name or a label, we put it into the box that has its name on it. We remove some of its wonder to us.

Come with me. You walk across a field and see these incredible, magical, free spirits fluttering around. They are extraordinarily beautiful. They fill you with joy, wonder and delight. You gaze in awe at them.

Then someone tells you they are butterflies. Now, they are labelled. You can look at them and know they are butterflies. Some of their magic has gone. You look at them without having to wonder or think. You think butterflies and march on. No need to indulge in them.

And we do this with people. Here is Jane, Mary, Abdul, Sam, and we know what to expect. We shut off parts of our processing. We look at them and respond to them with our head, not our heart.

We write our names in the sand: and then the waves roll in and wash them away.

Neil Gaiman

Mistakes

All bad behaviour is really a request for love, attention or validation.

Kimberly Giles

Why do we repeat the same mistakes over and over again? Why do we do things that are not in our best interests and repeat them? Why do we put up with the behaviour of others when their behaviour, if not abusive, is certainly inconsiderate? Why do we let people stifle us with love when the very stifling negates the love?

Maybe all of those are much too 'loud' for you to identify them in your life. And even if you do not suffer with any of them, if you're honest, you know people suffering because of them.

One of our challenges is that we hate to do anything to change the status quo, so we go along with things far longer than can possibly be good for us or make sense.

This is a call to arms. This is a challenge. It is a gentle nudge that you do something.

This is lifting the keyhole cover so that the tiniest ray of light can shine through, and we can realise it is possible to change. It may be challenging or uncomfortable, but it is possible. Be brave. Live a little more.

It is easy to remove a weevil from a grain, but hard to reverse the damage it does.

Michael Bassey Johnson

It's not a person's mistakes which define them – it's the way they make amends.

Freya North

Honesty

The secret of life is honesty and fair trading. If you can fake that, you've got it made.

Groucho Marx

Are you honest?
Are you honest with others?
Are you honest with yourself?

Most people have created a fiction in which they live comfortably enough. They never, or very rarely, lift the corner of the rug that conceals the truth about themselves.

And you might argue that is the right way to be. 'For god's sake, don't ask Mary how she is. She will tell you!'

However, we want to have at least one person in our life who knows what's under the rug. If we don't, it may fester, grow and destroy us.

Honesty opens the door to peace. Peace allows us to live.

There's just some magic in truth and honesty and openness.

Frank Ocean

Nothing is easier than self-deceit. For what every man wishes, that he also believes to be true.

Demosthenes

Action

Alone we can do so little; together we can do so much.

Helen Keller

Hey, what have you got planned today? It's so easy to get swept away with the same old, same old, going through it on autopilot.

And on the odd moment, we get away from the routine, we search for ways to indulge or amuse ourselves.

Here's an idea that will bring light into your day, life, and being.

Do something unexpected for someone else. Or make contact with someone you are out of touch with.

To achieve happiness is to give or bring joy to someone else. That's what makes us happy. Waiting for something else or someone else to make us happy does not work.

If you want to lift yourself up, lift up someone else.

Booker T Washington

May 20

Thoughts

If we were all on trial for our thoughts, we would all be hanged.

Margaret Atwood

We think.

A lot of the time, we think without ever doing anything to control our thoughts. They fly in and flit out, 60-80 thousand per day!

Some of them create little explosions of emotion in us. And we expand or reject the feeling without being aware that we are doing it.

We do not take control. We may not even imagine that we could be in control.

But with minimal effort, we can, if we choose, control our thoughts. We can deliberately discard the negative ones. We can enhance and live with the positive ones.

It's incredibly easy.

If we do it.

Man is a product of his thoughts, what he thinks, he becomes.

Mahatma Gandhi

Thoughts don't become things; thoughts ARE things.

Erics Micha'el Leventhal

Choice

If you want to sing out, sing out
And if you want to be free, be free
'Cause there's a million things to be
You know that there are.

Cat Stevens

If you want to be happy, be happy. If you want to be alive, be alive.

It is so easy to trudge through our day, eyes down, focusing on the puddles. Those pools of dirty, no filthy water, just waiting to pull you down deeper into their open arms.

There are times when we feel that we have no choice. We are locked into a lifetime of despair.

Maybe none of that applies to you. But have there ever been moments in your life when the blackness descended on you, even if you cannot fully remember it now?

And the lesson? Whether we are currently 'in it' or not, is that we have a choice.

We really do. We have a choice. We can choose peace regardless of what we are going through.

We have a choice. We do.

Well, if you want to say yes, say yes
And if you want to say no, say no
'Cause there's a million ways to go
You know there are.

Cat Stevens

May 22

Focus

The secret to staying young is to live honestly, eat slowly and lie about your age.

Lucille Ball

I cannot believe that you have got this far in your life without hearing, 'What you say is what you get,' or some variation on that theme.

What we focus on is what we bring into our life.

And yet... while we know this... do we do it? Do we praise ourselves, saying things like, 'I'm fit, healthy, energetic and beautiful.'

Or do we say things like, 'I'm too fat, unfit, I don't feel well, where has my energy gone?'

It applies to every area of our life. Our home, work, family and friends, and how we perceive and praise or criticise them.

But let's focus on ourselves, our bodies, health and fitness today.

Let's only talk good.

'I'm fit and healthy today, and I love my body. It is the perfect shape. I am beautiful and love myself.'

All the time, every day for the rest of your life.

It's not a big ask, surely.

Love yourself first and everything else falls into line.

Lucille Ball

Conflict

*Selfishness is not living as one wishes to live, it is asking
others to live as one wishes to live.*

Oscar Wilde

Think about being a child. It may be easier to think of a
child. Please think of how he/she is when they don't want to
do something. When they are determined to have their own
way. Because they know they are right, and come what may,
they are not budging. 'No!'

You get the picture. The posture, the clenched muscles,
the utter determination not to let go or change, the pure
wilfulness.

That child is still alive and well and living inside you.
(Inside me, too.)

That wave of knowing that we are right and will defend
what we think floods through our whole being. It is often just
a ripple, but a ripple or wave is the same. I'm tempted to say
it has self-righteousness to it, but perhaps that is too harsh.

However, it is not our friend. It is a close relation of anger
and harms us, just as anger does.

We do not want or need to be right. We want and need
peace.

We can discard our need to be right and replace it with
peace. We can choose peace. Everything changes. The battles
for rightness disappear, and we can live with peace.

*Peace is not the highest goal in life. It is the most
fundamental requirement.*

Sadhguru

May 24

Words

Thinking doesn't hurt. Words do. Words have the power to heal. Words have the power to kill.

Anne Maledon

My daughter would always spill her drinks. Whenever I placed a glass of water as we sat down to eat, I'd say, 'Don't spill it.' And she would.

I was told to stop saying that, instead, say, 'Here's your drink.'

It was that simple. She stopped spilling it.

Another thing my daughter had was a very messy room. I was constantly telling her how untidy it was. I started to say things like, 'You love a tidy room'. And 'Wow, your room is really tidy', and now, whilst it may not be the tidiest in the world, it is pretty good. And she does love a tidy room.

It works. Saying, focusing on what we want works. It happens. The unconscious obliges.

Life isn't about just talking, it's about thinking too.

Marie Symeon

Relationships

It is not your job to fix other people. You can't fix them. You can only change the way you live and the way you respond to life. Decide instead to have all the traits you wish to see in others, then you will generate your own brand of happy.

Lisa Prosen

Who is the most significant influence in your life? Who do you obey the most? Who do you jump the highest for, your parent or your partner?

And if you are in a 'good' relationship, should the answer not be your partner?

Or is your life filled with the constant need to please your parent?

So many of us fail to move on from the strings that bind us to our mother or father because, in our mind, we can never live up to the expectations we believe they have for us.

While some of us have shifted the certainty of personal failure from our parent to our partner, ensuring that in some area, we will fail.

Are you making the right choices about how and why you do things?

No person has the right to rain on your dreams.

Martin Luther King Jnr

It is not the load that breaks you down, it's the way you carry it.

Lou Holtz

Reality

The difference between fiction and reality? Fiction has to make sense.

Tom Clancy

Since we cannot change reality, let us change the eyes which see reality.

Nikos Kazantzakis

I was sitting in my living room looking at the river when a cormorant suddenly appeared from the depths with a fish in its mouth. It shook the fish three or four times, presumably to get it into the correct position, then it swallowed it and, without a glance at the world, dived back into the water.

Barely a second later, a seagull arrived, plucked something from the water and vanished as quickly as it came.

When I see things like that, I imagine a fish swimming along, chatting with its sister, and suddenly, she disappears. No warning. No explanation. One minute, sister. The next minute, nothing. Was she actually here, or did I imagine...?

Do we need explanations, or could we think, 'Oh, she's gone.'

Might life be better that way?

Is that the reality of this world?

Do we make too much of a meal out of it all?

Everything you can imagine is real.

Pablo Picasso

May 27

Self-Love

You've got to love yourself first. You've got to be okay on your own before you can be okay with someone else.

Jennifer Lopez

Do you love you?
Do you love yourself?
Please look in the mirror and say, 'I love you.'
Do it every day.
For a week.
Keep repeating this until you can believe and accept it.
Or better still, for the rest of your life.
Really look.
Really love.
You deserve love.
You deserve your love.
Get used to it.

To love yourself right now, just as you are, is to give yourself heaven. Don't wait until you die. If you wait, you die now. If you love, you live now.

Alan Cohen

May 28

Sleep

I love to sleep. Do you? Isn't it great? It is really the best of both worlds. You get to be alive and unconscious.

Rita Rudner

Would you like to go to sleep more easily? Here's something I picked up along the way.

Stop watching TV, your phone, etc., an hour before bed. (The messages will still be there in the morning, the world won't end, and if it does, you won't care anyway.)

Start with some long, slow breathing, then think of three things you have achieved today and how they benefited others. (They don't have to be massive world-altering, little things are fine.)

Next, think of three things you want to achieve tomorrow. Again, they don't have to be big things. Just something that you know that you can and will do tomorrow.

Finally, embrace a happy memory or the memory of something you are proud of. It can be recent or from any moment in your life.

Then sleep.

I love sleep. My life has a tendency to fall apart when I'm awake, you know?

Ernest Hemingway

You know you're in love when you can't fall asleep because reality is finally better than your dreams.

Dr Seuss

May 29

Enlightenment

Your own self-realisation is the greatest service you can render the world.

Ramana Maharshi

Budha was enlightened. Jesus was enlightened. To name just a couple. By and large, we feel that enlightenment is only available to the select few, the giants of history.

However, enlightenment is available to all of us at any time. We just have to let go and claim it. It may only be fleeting, but it is there.

We can experience the truth and the peace that goes with it. We can find ourselves knowing and saying things which, when we think about later, we realise that we would never have known or said under normal circumstances.

That is a flash of enlightenment. A time when you got out of the way and let the truth out.

You can do it if you get out of the way more often.

The true value of a human being can be found in the degree to which he has attained liberation from the self.

Albert Einstein

May 30

Worry

Worry is a thin stream of fear trickling through the mind. If encouraged, it cuts a channel into which all other thoughts are drained.

Arthur Somers Roche

Just think for a moment of some worry you've had recently. An event that has happened that you spent hours or even days worrying about. If you can, remember all the dreadful outcomes you created in your head.

And tell me honestly now, did any of the bad things come to pass?

They seldom happen.

And yet, our ego tortures us with endless potential disaster after disaster, thudding repeatedly in our minds.

Why do we do that?

If we step back and look at the ego and its idiocies, it stops. It can't do them when we watch it.

Surely, there is something we could learn there to make our journey through life more comfortable.

You're only here for a short visit. Don't hurry, don't worry. And be sure to smell flowers along the way.

Walter Hagen

May 31

Choice

The quality of your life is built on the quality of your decisions.

Wesam Fawzi

Hey, are you "less happy" than you'd like to be?

What are you thinking about that is causing you to feel "less happy"? You must be thinking about it, to be creating "less happy" in you.

And if that isn't happening now, I'm delighted, but keep the idea of this writing and use it one day when you do feel "less happy".

For you to be feeling it, you must be thinking about it. So, choose something else to think about.

It is that easy. It will create instant change. You do not have to think about things that you do not like.

That may seem like an outrageous idea, but it is true.

Do it and enjoy the freedom you choose.

No choice is the wrong choice as long as you make a choice. The only wrong choice is choosing not to make one.

Jake Abel

Enjoying?

Please

share

and

review

June 1

Self-Care

Caring for your body, mind, and spirit is your greatest and grandest responsibility. It is all about listening to the needs of your soul and then honouring them.

Kristi Ling

My body, your body, are temples. And they are the only ones we are getting this time around.

(If we return, we may get a new body to play with. If we don't, it won't bother us anyway.)

So anyway, we are what we've got. And at times, we forget that and cruelly mistreat it.

It is worth being mindful of what we eat, how we exercise, and how we pamper it. And it makes sense to indulge ourselves positively in all areas. It is not a luxury. It is common sense.

What we put into our minds makes a massive difference. Keep it positive.

Despite everything, life is full of beauty and meaning.

Etty Hillesum

Paranoia

Call me paranoid. I'm frequently right.

Seanan McGuire

My paranoia wasn't always right, but just to be on the safe side, I never went to sleep with a clown in my room.

Mark Henwick

Ah, that cheerful companion paranoia. I remember way back when, in the depths of my insanity, thinking to myself, 'Just because I am paranoid, it doesn't mean they aren't following me.'

I sat under the dining room table to roll joints because I believed that people were spying on me through the windows.

Who is this lunatic that is writing this stuff in this book? Why am I reading it?

I got sober. I found that it was possible to have peace of mind and love in my life. I threw myself into a recovery program, and I am so happy that I was invited to contribute to this book.

Happiness is available. It is not a myth.

Your mind is working at its best when you're being paranoid. You explore every avenue and possibility of your situation at high speed with total clarity.

Banksy

June 3

Self-Care

Physical fitness is not only one of the most important keys to a healthy body, it is the basis of dynamic and creative intellectual activity.

John F Kennedy

Walk a little further.

When you are going anywhere, choose the longer route. If you sit at a desk, find more excuses to move around.

Taking 15 minutes of exercise in the morning makes a difference to the whole of your day. And at the end of the day, you will have more energy left over to do the things you enjoy.

Climbs stairs. Avoid lifts. Walk up escalators. Walk slightly faster.

Move.

Move about.

Become liberated.

Enjoy.

Think with your whole body.

Taisen Deshimaru.

June 4

Living

You gotta walk that lonesome valley.
You gotta walk it by yourself.
Oh, nobody else can walk it for you.
You gotta walk it by yourself.

The Kingston Trio

That's it. We've just got to do it.

Yes, yes, of course, we can have help. We do, and we will, from others and our inner being. But in the final analysis, it is our journey, ours alone, and we have to take it.

And take it we will.

And as long as we keep going, we will come out the other side.

So we can take heart from that and get on with it, secure that it will all happen in one way or another. We do not need to fight it. We want to accept it.

Acceptance makes it so much easier.

Knowing only the valley is half wisdom; knowing only the hills is half wisdom; for full wisdom, know both the valley and the hills! Walk down and walk up!

Mehmet Murat ildan

June 5

Now

Make 'now' the primary focus of your life.

Eckhart Tolle

It is so easy to go through our day and life without genuinely experiencing most of it.

Living more of our life in the past or obsessing about all the things that will go wrong in the future.

So much so that we fail to enjoy or even notice what is happening now. What we're feeling, tasting, touching or looking at.

Abandon the past. There is nothing you can do about it. The future will happen exactly as it will, so stop fretting.

Throw yourself into the magic of the moment you are in.

Going back into the past to fix yesterday's negative memories is like trying to blow out an electric light bulb.

Sydney Banks

To live in the present moment is a miracle.

Thich Nhat Hanh

June 6

Unexpected

You have to take risks. We will only understand the miracle of life fully when we allow the unexpected to happen.

Paulo Coelho

Delight at the unexpected. Clap your hands in thanks and praise for it. Even if it is genuinely awful, be grateful for it.

There is nothing, absolutely nothing, worse than going through your day or life without encountering the unexpected.

To live in that drudge is not to be alive.

When people encounter anything out of the ordinary, many throw up their hands in horror, dashing back to the featureless hole they live in as quickly as possible.

So, be filled with joy when things happen. Even if, as you're making a cake, you discover all your eggs are rotten. Put the making on hold. Go to the shop filled with the excitement of getting new ones. You have been presented with the gift of the unexpected.

Revel in it.

The unexpected is what makes life possible.

Ursula K Le Guin

Who is afraid of something unexpected usually attracts fear further.

Radapar

Suffering

*I felt very still and empty, the way the eye of a tornado
must feel, moving dully along in the middle of the
surrounding hullabaloo.*

Sylvia Plath

If we feel empty, if we feel pain because we are not with
the person we love, nothing outside ourselves can genuinely
change that.

Okay, so we wouldn't feel the pain if they were here. But
them being here is just a distraction that temporarily fills the
hole until we are parted again.

If we are suffering because the person isn't with us, rather
than focusing on that pain and increasing it, we want to feel
joy that our love for someone is so great. Feel joy at their
existence.

The only permanent solution to any pain is within
ourselves.

If the person we love has died, remember with joy and
delight what you did together. Be filled with joy that you
knew them and shared love.

Be happy with your memories. Don't dive into sorrow.
They do not want you to suffer. Look at the beauty around
you and share what you see with them with happiness.

*Do not look for happiness outside yourself. The awakened
seek happiness inside.*

Peter Deunov

Struggles

May the fleas of a thousand camels invade the crotch of the person that ruins your day. And may their arms be too short to scratch.

Keisha Keenleyside

Trouble and strife. Struggles. Situations. Difficulties. Life.

We battle along like an uncorked bottle bobbing in the waves on the seashore, one little splash after another, filling us until we finally sink or are left high and dry on the beach.

No one said life was going to be easy. Did they?

But here's the thing, in any situation we find ourselves struggling with, we have three choices.

The first is to change it. Change what we do within it. Change how it goes.

The second is to walk away from it. Just leave.

And the third is to accept it completely. Accept that this is how it is (at the moment) and get on with it.

Choosing one of those and then going with that decision removes the stress we are inflicting on ourselves when we believe we have no control over it.

All Strife passes in time.

C A A Savastano

Gratitude

Happiness cannot be travelled to, owned, earned, worn, or consumed. Happiness is the spiritual experience of living every minute with love, grace, and gratitude.

Dennis Waitley

We take so much for granted. Going through our day, our lives without giving thanks for our multitude of blessings.

Food, transport, clean water, safe streets, a roof, a bed, and the air we breathe.

All accepted as being what we expect without a thought.

And yet...

Let's look at the universally available one. The ability to breathe. (It must be important; people keep mentioning it in meditations.) We do it without thought.

And yet... for some, that is not easy. I used to have asthma, and in 2002, I stopped breathing. I could no longer get the air into my lungs. I died. The next day, the doctor who'd saved me said I was her miracle.

So, I am grateful for the air and that I can breathe it. Very grateful.

So much better than the alternative.

Apparently.

Breath is the finest gift of nature. Be grateful for this wonderful gift.

Amit Ray

Meditation

The more regularly and the more deeply you meditate, the sooner you will find yourself acting always from a centre of peace.

J Donald Walter

No time to pray or meditate? No time for guidance?

Praying (to whatever) or meditating alters the whole time-space continuum.

That may be hard to believe, but praying or meditating alters our being, reactions, abilities, and thought processes. It purifies our mind. We have clarity of mind, and we have more time.

Meditation does not need to be a four-course meal with all the trimmings. It can be a few seconds of going inside ourselves, of handing the present moment over to God (if that is what you call it) and accepting guidance.

It removes the stress and the mental turmoil. It frees us to act with gentle certainty. It liberates us.

And, of course, the more often we do it, the easier it is. And the more benefit you get from it

If you know how to worry, you know how to meditate.

Joyce Meyer

Living

And if you get it like that
That's the way you get it
'Cause you get it like that
When you want to be that way
When you wanna be that way
That's the way you wanna be, see
Hey! It's alright

Van Morrison

Allow things to happen.
Accept them.
Don't fight, don't struggle.
If the message that you get comes from within, go with it.
We have two voices, the self-seeking lie from the ego and our instinct, the quiet certainty of our inner voice.
Listen, think, choose, decide and then act. But whatever you choose, do it wholeheartedly.
When you do something, do it fully. You cannot half jump out of a plane. You either jump or you don't. It is that simple.
Don't look back on your life with regret.
Have courage.

Decisiveness is a characteristic of high-performing men and women. Almost any decision is better than no decision at all.

Brian Tracy

Nothing is more difficult and therefore more precious, than to be able to decide.

Napoleon Bonaparte

June 12

Solutions

When I am working on a problem, I never think about beauty, but when I have finished, if the solution is not beautiful, I know it is wrong.

R Buckminster Fuller

There is always an easy solution to every problem – neat, plausible, and wrong.

H L Mencken

To find solutions to our challenges and problems, we want to let go of them. When we constantly battle with them, looking for answers, we become blinded by the details, and we become unable to see the forest for the trees.

Many successful people, including Einstein, talk about their breakthroughs, their answers come to them when they were doing something that takes them completely away from the problems, like sleeping.

It is good to practice letting go of things after we have done all the obvious things we can do and then step away. Do nothing or something completely unrelated to the challenge.

That is when you will receive the answers that you cannot find.

When the solution is simple, God is answering.

Albert Einstein

June 13

Nature

Look deep into nature, and then you will understand everything better.

Albert Einstein

All my life through, the new sights of nature made me rejoice like a child.

Marie Curie

It is easy to fill our day dashing from one task to another without stopping. And if we stop, we probably collapse in front of the TV and blast our poor soul with more disturbance.

Even if we manage to avoid the TV, when we are relaxing, we stay indoors, locked in our little box.

If we are lucky and have a garden, we can sit in that. If we can do that in silence, without our phone, it's good. Really good.

After all, we are animals from a world surrounded by nature, trees, plants and animals. Our soul benefits so much from even a little time spent out there.

Even better than collapsing in the garden is to walk, look, explore, discover, delight.

We return refreshed in a way that words cannot describe. We return with a feeling of oneness that truly nurtures us.

Forget not that the earth delights to feel your bare feet and the winds long to play with your hair.

Khalil Gibran

Solutions

Ride the horse in the direction that it's going.

Werner Erhard

So much of our life is spent trying to get the horse to go in the 'wrong' direction.

Yes, we may be absolutely sure we know the best direction, and 'if only' it would obey, everything would be perfect.

We are so stubborn and, dare I say it, foolish.

We yank and pull ourselves towards a mysterious goal that we are sure will solve our trouble. Desperately trying to do the 'right' things because we have been indoctrinated since birth!

However, there is the answer if we stop and go into the peace in our inner knowing and being. That is the direction we want to be choosing.

It is simple.

All you need to do to discover the answer is to do it.

When God wanted to create the horse, he said to the South Wind, 'I want to make a creature of you. Condense.' And the wind condensed.

Emir Abd-el-Kader

June 15

Self-Judgement

Once we accept our limits we go beyond them.

Albert Einstein

We are not perfect. Whether we have warts or not, accepting ourselves is so liberating.

We are not perfect.

But hey, who is the judge here? Who has decided what perfect is?

Is it possible that we, our ego, have created the idea of perfection? All our lives, we have seen people who are, apparently, better than us.

Yes, there may be one or two things we believe we excel at, but, well, they probably don't count anyway, do they?

So that's it then, we are doomed.

But let's thank God that is not true. We are so much more wonderful than we imagine. And we want to start believing that and applauding ourselves. Patting ourselves on the back for all the wonderful things we are and do.

Stop judging ourselves. Begin to be all the positive attributes we have.

Enjoy.

I want to be all that I am capable of becoming.

Katherine Mansfield

Resolve to be thyself: and know that he who finds himself, loses his misery.

Matthew Arnold

The only person who can pull me down is myself, and I'm not going to let myself pull me down anymore.

C Joybell C

June 16

Variety

Variety is the very spice of life, that gives it all its flavour.

William Cowper

Oh, how we yearn for variety, even when we don't realise it.

If someone compliments us frequently about how we look or something we've done, it quickly loses meaning.

We also need the bad things in life too. If we play a game and always win, we quickly get bored.

Anything we do repetitively quickly ceases to interest us unless we try to notice its little differences.

But one of the most important aspects of it is that when we are with others, we want to find different ways to engage with them and different compliments to use.

We want to be specific. 'You look lovely' probably does very little for them, whereas 'the way the colour in your earrings goes with your dress makes you look lovely' is a compliment that will mean something to them.

At work, find ways to praise people that are specific too. It will make all the difference to their productivity, sense of belonging and well-being.

Do things differently yourself. Travel by different routes. Focus on details as you travel. Do, eat, read, and watch different and unusual things.

Bring the light into your life.

People will forget what you said, people will forget what you did, but people will never forget how you made them feel.

Maya Angelou

Love

I like not only to be loved, but also to be told that I am loved... the realm of silence is large enough beyond the grave.

George Elliot

It is so vital to verbalise our love and affection to others. And to express our appreciation for the things they do.

We are not just talking about 'big' love here, we are talking about love for people in the world.

Love of the other people in the supermarket or the colleagues at work.

Finding some comfortable, appreciative words to say to them is so important.

Important to them and vital for us.

Love has nothing to do with what you are expecting to get – only with what you are expecting to give – which is everything.

Katherine Hepburn

Change

Change your life today. Don't gamble on the future, act now, without delay.

Simone de Beauvoir

If things are not going as well as we would like, we can change them if we have control over them.

So often, people complain about their 'lot' but do little or nothing to make any changes. So who's to blame, then?

If there are people in our lives who do not do what we (very reasonably) would like them to do, there is no point in complaining anymore. (Yes, anymore, because even if you haven't complained to them, you've bored others with your moaning.)

Let's accept this – we cannot change others by telling them what we want them to do. So, all we can do is change ourselves, our attitude, and our reactions to what they do or do not do.

I will not be afraid tomorrow, for I have seen yesterday and I love today.

William Allen White

Blame

*There is a luxury in self-reproach. When we blame
ourselves, we feel no one else has a right to blame us.*

Oscar Wilde

Many of us tend to blame other people for some of the
things in our life that we don't want.

We say or think things like 'Well, I do it because I have to'
or 'She made me' or 'This is what is expected of me' or
'Because they all do it'.

Of course, we may do things without even questioning
why we are doing them, with no idea that it might be
possible to choose what we do.

And bearing that in mind, it may be worthwhile to go
through your day observing yourself, watching what you are
doing and pondering 'Why'?

That could be the first step to liberation and a new way of
living.

*Don't blame the child for forgetting the lessons; make the
lessons unforgettable.*

Sonam Wangchuk

Time

The two most powerful warriors are patience and time.

Leo Tolstoy

Sometimes, we are overwhelmed with troubles, pain, depression or even their lesser brothers and sisters, and we feel swamped in a bog that has no horizon. It seems to stretch out endlessly before us with no way out.

But there is something more powerful than any of them, and that is time, if we hand over our troubles to it, they will change.

Everything changes when you put time into the equation. We know this if we dare to look.

Time changes everything; no one can stop it.

Ehsan Sehgal

Moving On

The problem with stress and anxiety is not that it happens, but more importantly, how long we hold on to it.

Andrew Johnson

We are constantly faced with challenges as we go through our day. Many we deal with and move on from, barely noticing them.

However, some we cling to, enlarge and intensify. There they are, boulders on ropes swinging from our necks and distorting our views and our world.

It is not the challenge that has done this. We have done it to ourselves. We have embraced all its difficulties and pulled them into our chest.

The event is 'out there'. Even if it is happening 'to us,' it is still out there. It is not part of us. We are not the challenge.

Step out of the challenge. Sever the rope and let the boulder crash away. Become yourself.

Then, with simple clarity, consider the challenge. It is different.

Accept yourself, love yourself, and keep moving forward. If you want to fly, you have to give up what weighs you down.

Roy T Bennet

Journey

Focus on the journey, not the destination. Joy is found not in finishing an activity but in doing it.

Greg Anderson

We never stand still. Our lives are journeys, and we are travelling through them. Even if we stop doing everything and give up, we are still not standing still.

We are just slowly sliding in the wrong direction. Everything is either growing or dying.

Everything.

So, to be healthy and happy, we want to move in a constructive direction.

We want to have goals. Even if they are tiny, even if they are magnificently unimportant, just knowing that we are going to have tea with Jane next Wednesday keeps our eyes looking up and ahead.

Even if all we plan to accomplish today is a pleasant exchange of words with the person at the shop, that is something.

Do not let yourself slide into being content with nothingness.

That path leads to death.

The bigger our goal, the more it consumes us, the better. But if you don't have a big goal, be sure that you have a small one. Life is a journey that must be travelled no matter how bad the roads and the accommodations.

Oliver Goldsmith

June 23

Lessons

So we shall let the reader answer this question for himself: who is the happier man, he who has braved the storm of life and lived or he who has stayed securely on shore and merely existed?

Hunter S Thompson

Surely there can only be one answer to that question?

And yet, when one is in the storm, complaining? Grasping? Fighting? Complaining? Wanting to give in? Complaining?

What then?

No one would choose this unless they were mad. Would they? No one could be stupid enough to choose this. They could not be so stupid.

And at the same time, crying out, 'I did not choose this!' 'I did not!' 'Save me from the insanity!' 'It is too much!' 'Much too much!' 'Make it go away!'

The only one who can make it go away is us. By travelling through it. By accepting its lesson.

And surely, the moment we realise this, the challenge changes. We can walk to the end of the tunnel where the light is.

Though we are so tempted to squeeze the end of the tunnel shut. To shut out the light. To succumb to our insane complaining.

A strange, stupid even, choice?

Life has become immeasurably better since I have been forced to stop taking it seriously.

Hunter S Thompson

June 24

Gratitude

*Acknowledging the good that you already have in your life
is the foundation for all abundance.*

Eckhart Tolle

Please take two or three long, slow, deep breaths.

Now, breathing normally, think of three things, one at a time, that you feel gratitude for. Go into them and really feel the gratitude.

They can be any three things, and they might just be that you can feel the air entering and leaving your body, that you can feel the aliveness and purpose that flows through you. That the world around you exists, with all its wonder.

Take as long as you need to find your three things, and then take another three long, slow, deep breaths.

From time to time to time, as you travel through your day, take long, slow, deep breaths and feel the gratitude as it flows through you. Filling you with love.

*Let us be grateful to the people who make us happy, they
are the charming gardeners who make our souls blossom.*

Marcel Proust

June 25

Oneness

When something is wrong with my baby,
Something is wrong with me.

Isaac Hayes & David Porter

When something is wrong with my baby, something is wrong with me.

It cuts through me like a rusty knife, tearing flesh as it goes.

How is it possible to have that kind of connectedness with anyone?

It is because we are all, you and me, one. We are connected at a spiritual level with everyone.

Most of the time, though, as we stumble blindly through our day, we do not tune into others. And often, because we are human, when people come to us with their troubles, without thinking, we tune out and stop listening after the first minute or two.

Do we do that because we are uncaring, because we fear overload, or just because we have enough of our own troubles?

If we can make the effort to stay connected with them, we will help them and ourselves.

Taking our eyes off ourselves lifts us and reduces any struggle we personally have.

its amazing how we are the composite of everyone we have ever met. it appears to me as of late that we are interwoven with people.

stephen christian

June 26

Denial

When people will not weed their own minds, they are apt to be overrun by nettles.

Horace Walpole

Quite often, we refuse to acknowledge the things that are happening in our lives. We operate from the blinkered view that if we do not talk about it, then it does not exist.

We carry on, our eyes and minds averted, refusing to be drawn into anything that might make it a reality.

'If I ignore it long enough, perhaps it will go away,' 'It won't exist.'

As we read that, we know the idiocy of lying to ourselves.

Things do not go away unless they are faced and dealt with. And if we hide from them, their size increases as they gather more 'stuff' and roll effortlessly up the hill!

Courage!

Be brave!

Grasp your life and move ahead with quiet strength.

It is better to be a thorn in the side of a friend than an echo.

Ralph Waldo Emerson

Isn't it strange that we talk least about the things we think about most.

Charles Lindberg

If it is important to you, you'll find a way. If it's not, you'll find an excuse.

Ryan Blair

June 27

Experience

Experience is one thing you can't get for nothing.

Oscar Wilde

Life is like playing a violin solo in public and learning the instrument as one goes on.

Samuel Butler

In the same way, as an orchestra needs all its instruments (even the triangle that only beats out four notes in the whole piece of music), we need to experience all our emotions. We also need to go through all the highs and lows in our lives.

(I know when you've hit the fourteenth disaster in a row, you question whether you really need quite 'so' many.)

However, we only encounter joy to its fullest when we have struggled through the thickets to get there.

There are times when we feel devastated with sadness, but again, this is something that we need to experience and so should therefore want.

When we realise and accept this, it changes our overall experience of what life throws at us. It is here. It is meant to be here. So I can have peace and serenity about it, faith that it and everything is okay and necessary for our journey.

Never for the sake of peace and quiet, deny your own experience or convictions.

Dag Hammarskjold

A man who carries a cat by the tail learns something he can learn in no other way.

Mark Twain

Life

Don't walk in front of me... I may not follow.
Don't walk behind me... I may not lead.
Walk beside me... just be my friend.

Albert Camus

You will never be happy if you continue to search for what happiness consists of. You will never live if you are looking for the meaning of life.

Albert Camus

It is so easy to waste our lives walking in front of others.
It is so easy to walk behind them, mindlessly following.
For enrichment. For joy. To truly live, we want to find a way to walk beside them.
As equals. Without demand.

Man is the only creature who refuses to be what he is.

Albert Camus

June 29

Uniqueness

Today you are you!
That is truer than true!
There is no one alive,
Who is you-er than you!

Dr Seuss

People say things like, 'You can never put your foot into the same river twice,' and we tend to think, 'Yeah, yeah, so what.'

And even if we don't think that, do we ever consider the implications of the opening statement?

No one has ever been where we are now, at this very moment. And no one will ever do it again.

Every second we experience is unique.

How we behave in it is genuinely significant. Everything we do alters the course of the future. Everything does. There is no going back.

So let's unbuckle our seat belts and throw ourselves into the fantastic adventure that is our life.

Don't let us be puddings, quietly rotting away in the chair. Let's be magic. Let's add meaning to the changes we are making in the world every second.

Enjoy.

Why fit in when you were born to STAND OUT?

Dr Suess

God

*I'm God. My belief system doesn't support a creator as such,
as we can call God, who created us in His/Her/Its image...
It's a hard question because I said at the start, I think we
invented God. So if I believe in God, and I do, it's because I
think I am God.*

Morgan Freeman

I believe that God dwells inside us all.

When we turn inward and find the voice and the answers
that are not the angry ego voice, we are talking to God.

We have a still, quiet wisdom.

We have peace.

We are at one with God.

And if we choose to move through our day accepting and
radiating peace and love, secure in our understanding that
we are God, the world changes. Our perception changes.

Everything changes. We are all God.

I am God.

Peace and Love.

*God is beyond all forms of life, but also indwells every form
of life as their essence. God is both beyond and within.*

Eckhart Tolle

*The universe is God. I am God, so that means I am the
universe.*

Oscar Wilde

Don't
Complain

Don't
Explain

Lessons

We cannot solve our problems with the same thinking we used to create them.

Albert Einstein

Some people, or should that be many people, constantly go over the things in their lives. They talk endlessly about them to anyone unfortunate enough to listen. Often just to themselves.

They hate and beat themselves for all their failures, shortcomings and wickedness.

Here's what we want to remember, we are here to learn.

Also, when we do something, or something is done to us, and we do not learn its lesson, the lesson is repeated.

Spoiler alert, it is repeated as many times as necessary until we learn the lesson.

And so... this is the significant part of this message... It is pointless to think about it anymore. It is just a negative drain.

Either we have learnt what we need to learn from it – or we haven't.

Either way, there is no point in thinking about it anymore.

Get on with your life.

Live.

For your sake, live.

The measure of intelligence is the ability to change.

Albert Einstein

July 2

Thoughts

I will no longer mutilate and destroy myself in order to find a secret behind the ruins.

Hermann Hesse

So here you are, sitting at a table with two glasses in front of you. One is the purest, most beautiful, vibrant spring water. The other is a slow, noxious poison. You can almost see the fumes rising from it.

So which do you drink?

It's your choice, a completely free, no-pressure choice.

Before you decide, let's be clear, we all have bad things that have happened to us or that we have done. Shitty, evil, unspeakable, unforgivable, you choose the word to describe yours.

Every time (I will repeat that in case you didn't get it), every time we think about any of these negative things, we are choosing to drink the poison. To poison ourselves. It doesn't poison the others involved in the event, only us.

If we want to poison ourselves, all we have to do is 'think' about any of them. Just think.

It is your thought that does it.

The way to change it is to forgive. Forgive them. Forgive yourself.

Forgive. Learn to love. To love yourself and them.

When god desires to destroy a thing, he entrusts its destruction to the thing itself. Every bad institution of this world ends by suicide.

Victor Hugo

Change

Everyone has a history. What you do with it is up to you. Some repeat it. Some learn from it. The really special ones use it to help others.

J M Green

So there you have it. You can stop now and consider your next step. And all the ones that follow it. Will they be wasted? Or magical?

It is up to you.

And just because, to date, we have wasted a lot of opportunities, it does not mean that we have to continue in the same way.

The choice – is ours.

Vision with action is merely a dream. Action without vision just passes the time. Vision with action can change the world.

Joel A Barker

One person can make a difference, and everyone should try.

J F Kennedy

July 4

Personalities

We have many separate selves that are all pursuing their own agendas.

There is the one that wants to be fit or eat less. At the same time, another wants to sit and watch TV and eat cake.

Another wants us to be angry or selfish, and at the same time, part of us is longing for peace and quiet.

And maybe by recognising that we have these different selves, we can move through them and into our hearts and inner being, which is who we truly are.

July 5

Change

For the last month or so, I have suffered from a bad knee and leg. Shooting pains and nights of sitting up because lying down has been too painful.

Today, I woke up, and it is better than it has been for ages. I do not know why. I guess it has run its course.

Years ago, I had sciatica, with overwhelming and immobilising pain. The only good thing was occasionally meeting others who said they had had sciatica, too. And they clearly no longer did.

I know that when we're in the midst of challenges and pain, either mental or physical, the idea that it will pass is far too big a notion for us even to contemplate. And yet, every experience we have had, good or bad, has changed.

This one, whatever we are going through, will change too.

One day it will be alright.

That I can promise you, however unbelievable that may seem today.

Everyone goes through difficult times, but it is those who push through those difficult times who will eventually become successful in life. Don't give up, because this too shall pass.

Jeanette Coron

Thoughts

Thought is not written in stone. It is fluid and can be moulded to suit the day.

Sydney Banks

So often, we are trapped by our merry-go-round of thoughts. Perhaps that should be, 'by our not very merry-go-round of thoughts'.

They swirl around in our head, apparently uncontrollably. And even when we are not looking at one specific dark thought, we are aware of the black gloom because all our thoughts appear overwhelming.

Our cry of 'I feel so depressed' is not unleashed by one thought but by the collective ghastliness of everything.

And yet, we have control over our thoughts. We choose them.

If we choose to change our focus, everything else changes too.

If we choose to look.

If we choose to look at nature in its wonder and smile.

If we choose to think with love and smile.

If we indulge in peace and smile.

The negative moves over to make way for the positive.

It is our choice.

We do choose what we think of.

You don't have to control your thoughts. You just have to stop letting them control you.

Dan Millman

July 7

Phones

Eyes, ears, nose, and brain glued to the screen. Mind dancing to the unreality of our phone, with its 'anti-social' media, devouring us.

I watch people walking down the path on the other side of the river, their heads bent over their phone. Unaware of life.

Oblivious to their toddlers who run around them, pointing out and discovering the wonders in the world.

It is too easy to be captured by the lies our phones spew.

Of course, it is our choice.

We do not need to be consumed by it.

If we think we need to indulge, then that is another lie we use to excuse ourselves.

Love

If you have the ability to love, love yourself first.

Charles Bukowski

For many, the notion of loving oneself is all wrong. They push the idea away.

And yet, when we respect, value and love ourselves, the world opens. Our ability to love and be of use to others is revealed.

When we take care of ourselves and refuse to allow the disregard others have for us to affect us, we become valuable. We become real.

Some of you cry out, 'But I do love her/him' and 'I love this or that.'

But that is secondary. Until we learn to love ourselves, we cannot truly love others or other things. The door to love is slammed shut. Discover the wonder that unfolds when you open it.

Then, we can breathe in the gentle joy of being alive.

How you love yourself is how you teach others to love you.

Rupi Kaur

Living

This life chose you, and it's happening right now.

Lauren Lee

Somehow, realising that this life chose me changes it.

It changes how I go about my life.

The one thing that is painfully obvious is that too many of us take life far too seriously.

Taking things seriously takes the glitter from it.

Laughing at ourselves, others and our situations is so important. It liberates us from our challenges.

Some things we are doing or are involved in will go badly. Many of them will go well.

But whichever way they go, we will look back on them in the future, and they will matter far less than they do now.

So, realise this now.

Realise that nothing is as important as we think. It will pass. So, choose to move into that process now. Let go. Get on with enjoying your life.

Letting go means to come to the realisation that some people are a part of your history, but not a part of your destiny.

Steve Maraboli

Life

Life is a gift. Never take it for granted.

Sasha Azevedo

It's horribly easy to go through our day, week, or month without gratitude.

Without ever stopping to think that our life is a gift.

Just marching or perhaps scrabbling through our day without thought.

Struggling through the next thing that 'must' be done.

So sad.

And unnecessary.

Stop for a few moments and realise what we are experiencing is a gift. Take long enough to say, 'Thank you,' then take the empowerment our gratitude gives us, to step into the next moment with courage and even joy.

There is a beautiful rainbow awaiting your arrival down the road, with all the celebration and glamour. Get ready.

Hiral Nagda

Tolerance

Ninety per cent of the art of living consists of getting along with people you cannot stand.

Samuel Goldwyn

If there are people in our lives whom we constantly find fault with in one way or another, we often search for others who share our opinions.

We want them to dislike the culprit as much as we do. We want to share our little (or big) niggles about them.

The trouble with this is we are searching for the negative. It creates a negative expectation about people around us. And it grows. So, it infects our thinking and behaviour. This poisons us, which is, to put it mildly, a shame.

If we can change our outlook to the positive and look for the good things, then our interactions become an opportunity for us to practice tolerance.

And we may also look at our interactions as opportunities to learn things.

Our world would undoubtedly be bland if everything in it was exactly how we wanted it to be.

If you cannot get along with yourself, you will never be able to get along with other people.

Joel Osteen

July 12

Beliefs

Whatever may befall you, it was preordained for you from everlasting.

Marcus Aurelius

Some people believe that before we arrive here on earth, we look at the life we will lead and agree to it.

To most people, that probably seems far-fetched, but entertain for a moment that it might be true.

It means that all the things we have been through and survived were planned.

And all the things to come have also been planned.

It is liberating. It takes away a lot of struggle and worry. It frees us to get on with our life, doing the best we can, but no longer crippled by the anxiety of the future.

There is no wrong way for reality to play out.

Charlotte Eriksson

July 13

Struggles

You start with a darkness to move through, but sometimes the darkness moves through you.

Dean Young

Everyone is struggling in some way and has difficulties they are going through. (The challenges in this world are not only reserved for you.) We all have them.

And when people are being challenged, they sometimes behave badly. Like a child not getting its own way, they kick, scream, hit, and bite. They withdraw and sulk, they...

Our natural response is to react badly to people who treat us badly.

Okay, the grown-up behaviours may look more sophisticated. But it all comes down to the same thing.

But if we remember that they are having a hard time, and that's why they're behaving like that, it is easier to step back.

Not to take it personally. Help them if we can. And certainly not to do anything that will increase their unwarranted behaviour, which is a cry for help.

No matter how bad things are, you can always make things worse.

Randy Pausch

July 14

Change

And you think you can't change the universe? I say, think again. You are its only possibility.

Karen Casey

Be kind.
Be loving.
Spread love and kindness. They are contagious.
Be kind to everyone.
As Mother Teresa says, 'Start with the person standing next to you.'
Make it a goal that every person you speak to or meet goes away feeling better having been in your company.
Focus on the good things.
Share.
Enjoy.

Never doubt that a small group of thoughtful, committed citizens can change the world. Indeed, it is the only thing that ever has.

Margaret Mead

Addiction

*There are all kinds of addicts, I guess. We all have pain.
And we look for ways to make the pain go away.*

Sherman Alexie

Addiction is a lie.

We don't think that. We think it's the answer, whether our addiction is drugs or drink. Or whether, far more commonly, our addiction is shopping, food, TV, gaming, exercising, gambling (please add your own to the list).

They are all lies. They promise us some kind of relief or release, but they break their promise. Because once we have eaten, bought, played, drugged ourselves, our addiction says, 'That didn't work! Do it again! Now! Hurry! Hurry!'

So addiction is a lie.

Perhaps, realising that, we can begin to reject it, rather than succumb to it?

Be nice to feel the gentle comfort and ease that flows through us as we refuse to indulge in the insanity.

The attempt to escape from pain, is what creates more pain.

Gabor Maté

"Wait for me." The words come out choked and pained. "I need you to wait for me."

Krista Ritchie (From 'Addicted to you')

Listening

Listening is a positive act. You have to put yourself out to do it.

David Hockney

Can you spare me a few moments, or rather, can you spare yourself a few moments? Start to breathe, in and out, long and slow, without pausing in between so that your breath becomes a circle.

Continue.

It doesn't matter if the length of the breath changes. Continue as you read without a pause at the top or bottom of the breath.

And as you continue, sink into yourself (not physically), but into your inner being.

Continue to breathe.

Circle.

Circle.

In and out, without pause.

Be inside.

Be yourself.

And listen, continue to breathe and listen.

Even if you have no question – listen.

Breathe and listen

Even if the answer has no words, listen and absorb it.

Breathe, listen, absorb.

I remind myself every morning: Nothing I say this day will teach me anything. So, if I'm going to learn, I must do it by listening.

Larry King

There is a difference between listening and waiting for your turn to speak.

Simon Sinek

Oneness

Mind cannot think without duality. Duality is the way of thinking. In silence, all dualities disappear.

Rajneesh

There can be no good without bad.
No fat, without thin.
No quiet, without noise.
Things only exist because their opposites exist.
We cannot suffer unless we experience non-suffering.
When we can accept that we have or have had peace and suffering and we go into the centre of them, they become one.

When we go into both simultaneously, we can have peace.

We are just travelling through our lives. When we claim the balance within, we experience the balance without. We are no longer available to pain. We are neither peace nor suffering.

All things pass. We shall pass. We shall become oneness again.

We can claim and experience oneness now whenever we stop indulging ourselves and choose oneness.

Just as we have two eyes and two feet, duality is part of life.

Carlos Santana

July 18

Self-Care

Loving yourself isn't vanity. It's sanity.

Katrina Mayer

I love my body as my own. I treat it with respect.

How many of us can say that or have even thought about it?

And if we are not doing that, then why?

It is the only one we get.

Is today the day to begin moving towards accomplishing this?

If not, why not?

Dare to love yourself as if you were a rainbow with gold at both ends.

Aberjhani

July 19

Being

Distance has the same effect on the mind as on the eye.

Samuel Johnson

Come on a journey with me. Stand on the beach and look at the power of the sea. Drive through the open countryside with mountains in the distance. Explore the dark ground and the intimacy of walking through a thick wood or forest.

And tell me, did you ever think to yourself, 'Is this all there is?'

Of course not.

And yet, in our lives, at times of struggle, pain and difficulty, we may easily fall into the trap of believing that this is all there is. Trapped forever in the disaster of it all.

We do not need to be tricked into thinking this is all there is.

The whole world is out there. We shall return.

But nothing makes a room feel emptier than wanting someone in it.

Calla Quinn

July 20

Subconscious

Never go to sleep without a request to your subconscious.

Thomas Edison

Our subconscious works away all the time, doing its best to create the reality that we believe in.

By making requests, by telling it what we want, we can guide it and ourselves into the reality we want.

So by saying to ourselves when we go to bed, 'Tomorrow, I shall be full of energy,' or ' I feel confident in my abilities,' or 'I can push through my wall easily when I'm running my marathon,' our subconscious or unconscious can prepare itself, and us, to achieve things easily when we might otherwise find them challenging.

You are a captain navigating a ship. You must give the right orders, thoughts and images to your subconscious, which controls and governs all your experiences.

Joseph Murphy

July 21

Living

Rather, ten times, die in the surf, heralding the way to a new world, than stand idly on the shore.

Florence Nightingale

Are you standing idly on the shore?
Why?

I never gave or took any excuse.

Florence Nightingale

Time

A man who dares to waste one hour of time has not discovered the value of life.

Charles Darwin

We are only here for such a short time.

We forget that and squander our moments. We lose sight of the good we could be doing because we chase our tails as we flit from one piece of rubbish to another.

If we were told today, that's it. Today's all you've got.

What, then, would we do?

Give and exchange love, I suspect. All the petty things would seem irrelevant.

Give and exchange love.

And if that is what we would do.

What are we doing?

We are only here for such a short time.

You may delay, but time will not.

Benjamin Franklin

Thinking

Not to be able to stop thinking is a dreadful affliction, but we don't realise this because almost everybody is suffering from it, so it is considered normal.

Eckhart Tolle

The washing machine head. That endless noise. Going on and on, endlessly!

Realising that others suffer from this helps, even if only a little.

The sad thing is we know how to stop it. We know we should breathe. We know we should go inside ourselves and find the peace and calm that is there.

We know it's easy to do.

But the idea of starting to do that is such an effort. And the other part of our mind is doing everything possible to prevent us.

Courage.

Determination.

Love.

A scream is always just that, a noise and not music.

Carl Jung

The worst wheel of the cart makes the most noise.

Benjamin Franklin

July 24

Mirror

Everybody else needs mirrors to remind themselves who they are. You're no different.

Jonathan Nolan

Look at yourself in a mirror. Look into your eyes. Look at your face. Long, slow, gently.
Say aloud...
'May I be well.'
'May I experience joy, peace and love.'
'I love you (say your name).'
'I love you.'
'I love you.'
Repeat at least three times.
Repeat daily for the rest of your life!
Enjoy.

I used to look in the mirror and feel shame. I look in the mirror now and I absolutely love myself.

Drew Barrymore

Smile in the mirror. Do that every morning and you'll start to see a big difference in your life.

Yoko Ono

July 25

Self-Doubt

Almost all of the ideas we have about being a man or being a woman are so burdened with pain, anxiety, fear and self-doubt. For many of us, the confusion around this question is excruciating.

Andrew Cohen

Think, if you will, of the most successful person you know or who you know of. Friend, celebrity, superstar, sports person, politician, religious leader, it doesn't matter what walk of life, choose one.

And let me tell you this truth about them. They have insecurities. They worry about whether what they are doing is right, could be better, or should have been done differently. They worry about what people think of them. And what their loved ones think about them. And whether they should have said or done that.

I know, I know, it's hard to believe. But it is true. Everyone has that critical, self-doubting inner voice.

Yes, everyone. You are not alone. And knowing that makes a difference.

I can't think of anyone I admire who isn't fuelled by self-doubt. It is an essential ingredient. It's the grit in the oyster.

Richard Eyre

July 26

Change

True friends don't come with conditions.

Aaron Lauritsen

If only he, she, they, the world would... If only they would...

It isn't as if I ask for much. But...

Shock horror!

The only person we can ever change is ourselves.

Sure, we can discuss things, we can get agreements. But until they choose to change, there ain't nothing we can do.

Oh, wait.

Oh yes, there is... we can choose to be at peace. We can allow others the right to be the way they are. We can share our love and peace with them.

And I promise you, when you do, they will start to explore and share love and peace with the world, too.

It may not happen as fast as we would like... but...

We can have quiet peace within ourselves.

The struggles we endure today will be the 'good old days' we laugh about tomorrow.

Aaron Lauritsen

Listening

When things are exceptionally hard, there is a reason why they are hard; and it's usually because they're not meant to be, and we are not listening.

Rachael Bermingham

Sometimes, people say, 'I don't know which voice is the ego and which is mine.' 'Who am I?' 'Which is my inner voice?'

The answer comes if we ask, 'Is what it's saying helpful?'

The ego (surprise, surprise) is not helpful.

It may (being well cunning) disguise itself as helpful, but it isn't. For example, when we want to do something we used to do easily, the ego will say, 'You used to be able to do that easily,' but it's subtext there is, 'But you can't anymore, you're useless.'

So there you go.

Is what you are saying to yourself helpful? Is it encouraging? Is it loving? If it is, it's your inner voice. If it's not helpful, ignore it and go and find the suggestions that come wrapped in love.

It takes patience to listen. It takes skill to pretend you're listening.

Harmon Okinyo

Change

True life is lived when tiny changes occur.

Leo Tolstoy

Sometimes, we cry out for change. Our existence, as it is, appals us. (Perhaps appals is too strong a word, but you know what I mean.) We cry out to ourselves, if not the world, that things have got to change.

And, more often than not, the task, the very idea of it, is so enormous that we do nothing.

We wait until tomorrow to cry out again, 'I must have change.'

Before once more doing nothing. Except maybe thinking a little less of ourselves. After all, it's another straw marked 'Failure!' that we are tossing onto our back.

So if we want, if we really want to change, let's give ourselves a break. Let's simplify it.

Choose one minuscule thing and change that. And continue with it until that becomes the way things are. Then, choose the next microscopic thing and do that.

Oh, and remember to pat yourself on the back as you achieve.

Not everything that is faced can be changed, but nothing can be changed until it is faced.

James Baldwin

Never too old, never too bad, never too late, never too sick to start from scratch once again.

Bikram Choudhury

Journey

A mind that is stretched by a new experience can never go back to its old dimensions.

Oliver Wendell Holmes

I'm continually coming across writings that say, in one way or another, that we are precisely where we are meant to be right now. So many diverse sources, all saying the same thing in their own way, that we are living through what we are supposed to be experiencing.

Such a vast number, one cannot help but believe that perhaps they know what they are talking about.

And if that is the case, if we are where we should be now, then that instantly lessens any burden we may be experiencing.

For whatever it is, it is meant to be. It will pass. We will move on. The erroneous feeling that we have that this will never end is just that, wrong.

Wherever you go, go with all your heart.

Confucius

Honesty

Strange how complicated we can make things just to avoid showing what we feel.

Erich Maria Remarque

We hide so much. We only let out little corners of the truth, lest we expose ourselves.

We ask for help, and yet we do not tell what is at the core of our trouble. Often, we may not know, so we invent bits of nonsense to keep others at bay.

The truth is inside ourselves, and yet we dare not sit in silence long enough to recognise it. The truth is what we hide.

We create our trouble with our thoughts about ourselves and others.

Allowing others to create a feeling of failure throughout us.

We are perfect as we are, and when we allow ourselves to float into that, there are no troubles.

The person we present to the world is a lie.

What they present to us are lies too.

Accepting ourselves as our true being gives us freedom. If we but dare.

It was a melancholy secret that reality can arouse desires but never satisfy them.

Erich Maria Remarque

July 31

Expectations

Expectation is the root of all heartache.

William Shakespeare

There are things that we know. We know what we will look like in those clothes. We know the kettle will boil. We know that the car will start.

One certainty after another.

None of them require any effort or emotion on our part.

We are only truly alive when we are involved in the new or processing the old as if it were new.

If we throw ourselves into life, it shines with a magnificent brightness. We deserve to be enveloped in that. We owe it to ourselves to be alive.

Awareness is like the sun. When it shines on things, they are transformed.

Thich Nhat Hanh

Your
thoughts
create
Your
reality

Habits

We are what we repeatedly do. Excellence, then, is not an act but a habit.

Aristotle

It is so easy to get out of the habit of doing things. Let's say on a Thursday night, you always go to the pub, bingo, line dancing, an AA meeting, to church, or to run a scout's group.

Then things happen, little things or big things, like the period of Covid isolation, and you stop going. You get out of the habit.

You're doing okay without it. Thursday comes along, and you think, 'No, I will give it a miss this Thursday. I'll definitely go next Thursday, though.'

Time passes, and Thursday becomes another stay-at-home-and-do-nothing day.

Big shame?

Change happens when the pain of staying the same is greater than the pain of change.

Tony Robbins

August 2

Existence

What happens to the hole when the cheese has gone?

Bertolt Brecht

My son asked me that question when he was seven.

I did not know the answer, but thinking about it now, I wonder, was the hole there before the cheese?

Sometime later, I was holding my father's hand when he died.

Something left him.

Something I can only describe as his soul because I do not know any better words.

What happened to his soul when he died?

I do not know. But I suspect that it continued its journey with other souls. Waiting perhaps to travel on into a new body.

Perhaps my son's hole is just waiting for a new cheese?

Do not fear death, so much as an inadequate life.

Bertolt Brecht

Courtesy

Courtesy, it is also currency. It pays to be lovely to people.

Janna Cachola

When I was young, my father would open the car door for my mother.

Simple courtesy.

(I know, women like to open the car door for themselves these days – and that's great – but that's not the point.)

It is so easy to be courteous. Let a car into the stream of traffic, move aside on the crowded pavement, get someone a coffee, and spend a few seconds making other people's lives easier.

And courtesy (like anger) is contagious. If we treat the world with respect and love, that is what flows out into the world.

Have fun. Seize the opportunities the world offers you.

As we are, so we do; and as we do; so it is done to us; we are the builders of our fortunes.

Ralph Waldo Emerson

Behaviour

'I heard you were dead.'

'I heard you wear a red lace corset.' I said matter-of-factly. But I don't believe every bit of nonsense that gets rumoured about.'

Patrick Rothfuss

We all know people we instantly mistrust or feel guarded when we are with them. People whom we don't tell things about ourselves that we might share comfortably with others. Our self-preservation warns us to keep away.

And that makes a lot of sense. Some gossips feed on other people's sufferings with delight. There are people at work whose self-interest would do anything it could to halt the progress of others.

And so we learn, hopefully, who to trust.

But here's a thought, a question we want to look at.

Are we ever nice, charming, and friendly with people and then when we leave them, we gossip and laugh about them?

Is that the kind of person you want to be?

Little people need to belittle.

Wayne Gerard Trotman

August 5

Self-Torture

*When you're unhappy, I guess everything in the world –
reading, eating, sleeping – has something buried
somewhere inside it that makes you unhappier.*

Nick Hornby

Spirals.

Going down.

Down, down, down.

And that appeals to us as we pull the duvet tighter around us to block out the world.

And yet, we know that this isn't our only state.

We have had better times. And if they existed, then they can again.

We do not have to dive straight back into the unadulterated joy. That would surely be too much to bear.

But if we can lift the corner of the duvet and look at the light. And think, 'Ah yes, light, I remember, that was nice.'

And then, maybe, just maybe, allow a little more light to shine into us.

We get what we focus on.

We choose. Light or dark. The pain will only continue for as long as we embrace it.

None of which will help until we are ready.

Obviously I faced the possibility of not returning when I first considered going. Once faced and settled, there really wasn't any good reason to refer to it.

Amelia Earhart (An American aviation pioneer)

Happiness

It isn't what you have, or who you are, or where you are, or what you are doing that makes you happy or unhappy. It is what you think about it.

Dale Carnegie

It is so easy to fall into the trap of making other people or things responsible for our happiness.

It gives them power and control over us. And if we could be honest about things or future events that we expect to provide us with happiness, we know that they cannot give us happiness.

Yes, we may get a fleeting buzz of joy from them, but all our experiences prove that it does not last. And the next time will not last either.

And so it is with people. Yes, we may love them and yearn to be with them. And we may have peace and happiness when we are with them. But it is not that which is making us happy.

We do happy with ourselves. If we love them and are not with them, we can still do happiness to ourselves because we can feel the love. They do not need to be here.

And if you look at relationships historically, it is almost certain that neither they nor their love will be here in the future.

So it makes sense to do happiness because you feel the love now. Especially when you are not together.

Sometimes, your joy is the source of your smile, but sometimes, your smile can be the source of your joy.

Thich Nhat Hanh

August 7

War

There have been only 268 of the past 3,421 years free of War.

Will Durant

Will Durant lived from 1885-1981, and I have not been able to find out exactly when he wrote that.
But somehow, it questions the sanity of man?
And now the war ravages Ukraine.
It makes one think, doesn't it?
Despair a little?

Those that fail to learn from history are doomed to repeat it.

Winston Churchill

If we don't end war, war will end us.

H G Wells

August 8

Handing over

Life is a series of natural and spontaneous changes. Don't resist them, that only creates sorrow. Let reality be reality. Let things flow naturally forward in whatever way they like.

Lao Tzu

When new things come into our lives, new jobs, new people, new relationships, we cannot begin to know where they will lead. At some level, we are travelling into the unknown, which can fill us with uncertainty and fear.

But that has been the case throughout our lives. Our whole life has been a process of going through endless doors, into darkened rooms, only to find that we can manage the new experience.

If we realise this, we will know that we can handle the new event. We are not alone. Nothing is too big for us. Remembering and trusting will make our journey easier.

Handing the experience over and knowing that everything is not up to us will empower us and enable us to have quiet acceptance.

You couldn't relive your life, skipping the awful parts, without losing what made it worthwhile. You had to accept it as a whole – like the world, or the person you loved.

Stewart O'Nan

August 9

Help

I tried to groan, Help! Help! But the tone that came out was that of polite conversation.

Samuel Beckett

Some of us find it very difficult to ask for help. We have trained ourselves to be independent. We are proud. We believe that asking for help is a sign of unspeakable weakness.

However, we are not meant to do it all by ourselves. We travel through this world together so that we can help each other. And so learn and be rewarded.

Bearing that in mind, asking for help is the right thing to do. It is by giving and receiving help that we grow.

One of the biggest defects in life is the inability to ask for help.

Robert Kiyosaki

August 10

Seeds

Anyone can count the seeds in an apple, but only God can count the number of apples in a seed.

Robert H Schuller

Do you remember as a child when you planted your first seed? Perhaps at school, in a yoghurt pot placed on a windowsill, then the waiting and hoping began.

How did it know which type of plant to become?

How could anything that tiny transform itself into a plant?

We all know, 'What we sow, we reap.' But do we ever stop to consider how it affects us?

If we love ourselves with compassion, that will grow and bloom. We want to feed ourselves with positive expectations.

We can become so much more with self-love.

You can't sow an apple seed and expect to get an avocado tree. The consequences of your life are sown in what you do and how you behave.

Tom Shadyac

Temptation

Lead me not into temptation, I can find the way myself.

Rita Mae Brown

The only way to get rid of temptation is to yield to it... I can resist everything but temptation.

Oscar Wilde

Yes, if we want to, we can say, 'No thank you' to the cake or some behaviour we'd rather not do. It may not be easy, but it is not impossible.

But the real, the dangerous temptations are the ones that we don't even notice. The ones that have just become a habit. Like the temptation to be sarcastic, to put someone down, to snap at someone with a brief flash of anger, to think less of them, to close ourselves away from them.

They are all temptations, and giving into them without a thought is so easy.

And then there are the times when we do not show our sympathy, that we care, that we love, that we want to be part of their life. Times when we just cannot be bothered to be interested or to listen.

We cannot be perfect. We cannot expect that. But we can be a whole lot better with a little effort and determination.

Always remember that you are absolutely unique. Just like everyone else.

Margaret Mead

Change

Incredible change happens in your life when you decide to take control over what you do have power over instead of craving control over what you don't.

Steve Maraboli

No one will change unless they want to. We cannot do it for them. They have to want to change themselves.

We want to learn to accept and let go for our peace of mind.

If we are doing things which enable them to continue their behaviour, we can stop. We can withdraw our support. It is not easy to do that, but as long as we carry on in the way we have, there will be no change.

And I am talking about everything here, all the way from picking up their socks, feeding them, or trying to throw their drugs away.

Nothing will change if we are in their life and continue to behave as we have.

We have to stop. That is why it is called 'tough love'. It is very hard for us to do, especially when we love them.

Even when we no longer love them.

If they will not change, then we will have to change.

If we can accept this, let go and find inner peace, then we will be available if and when they are ready to change.

To improve is to change; to be perfect is to change often.

Winston Churchill

The secret of change is to focus all of your energy not on fighting the old, but on building the new.

Socrates

Letting Go

Be soft. Do not let the world make you hard. Do not let pain make you hate. Do not let the bitterness steal your sweetness.

Kurt Vonnegut

In a flash, our reaction can change us from soft to hard. The accumulation of unjustness can obliterate our softness.

And that happens without our giving it a thought.

It need not.

We have a choice.

We can discard our cloud of bitterness or rage. We can choose soft.

Tell me. No, tell yourself, in what possible way does being hard help you?

Why are you entertaining the lie that your desire for revenge can possibly profit you?

Let go.

Smile.

Move on.

Be soft.

There is no revenge so complete as forgiveness.

Josh Billings

August 14

Choice

I am very little inclined on any occasion to say anything unless I hope to produce some good by it.

Abraham Lincoln

Does it need to be said?
Does it need to be said by me?
Does it need to be said by me now?
Good questions to consider.
If the answer to any of them is no, then don't say it.
We can't walk backwards from what we say or do. It is done.
Mind you, it is far better to say something than write it. Written stuff is there forever, waiting to be waived in the air!
I counsel caution.

Why talk and say the unsaid words in haste when silence can speak the unspoken words?

Ernest Agyemang Yeboah

August 15

Freedom

If you live your life a hostage to everybody else's decision, you either have to live a very narrow life, or you have to spend a lot of time in pain.

Newt Gingrich

So much of our security, identity, and peace of mind is tied to how we think our friends, partners, etc., view us. We need their approval, at some level, to feel okay about ourselves.

And often, we cling to them, demanding their attention and dictating their behaviour as much as possible. They have become our hostages whom we dare not release. If we did let them go, then we would cease to exist. Or so our ego tells us, manipulating both our life and theirs.

If we let go of the ego's viewpoint and move to the vision that our soul has, all our insecurities fall away. We can see them and ourselves with love. Travelling our paths, together or separately, with freedom.

We no longer crave their 'right' behaviour. We can experience love.

You can either be a host to God or a hostage to your ego. It's your call.

Wayne Dyer

Challenges

Don't feel sorry for yourself if you have chosen the wrong road, turn around.

Edgar Cayce

So often, things feel wrong, or at least they don't feel right, but we soldier on anyway.

We employ a builder to do some work, and although he keeps letting us down, we hope and expect it to all go okay in the end. And the longer we wait, the deeper the hole we find ourselves in.

It is better to go with the three strikes and you're out rule. If he/she can't keep their word, get rid of them. It doesn't matter if people laugh at you, have courage. Do it.

The builder example is just that, an example. Many things happen in our lives that go from bad to worse, but we plod on anyway.

Particularly if it is a family member, we end up bending over backwards, breaking our back, in the futile hope that it will change.

More often than not, they will not change, and we know that at a base level. But we continue anyway.

It is worth looking at the causes of the turmoil in your life and then having the courage to end them.

You cannot push a dead horse up a hill.

When things go wrong, don't go with them.

Elvis Presley

August 17

Self-Care

One day, you will wake up, and there won't be any more time to do the things you've always wanted. Do it now.

Paulo Coelho

When did you last have a day off? Come to that, have you ever had a day off? And what on earth would it be like?

I'm not going to make a single suggestion. It wants to be your day. What do you have to do, or not do, to accomplish it?

And even if a day is impossible for you now, how about an actual half day?

All work and no play makes Jack a dull boy.

Go and play for a day and feel the life energy flowing into you.

You're off to Great places! Today is your day! Your mountain is waiting! So... get on your way.

Dr Suess

There comes a day when you realise turning the page is the best feeling in the world, because you realise there is so much more to the book than the page you were stuck on.

Zayn Malik

Peace

I can have peace of mind only when I forgive rather than judge.

Gerald Jampolsky

How many goals do you have? How many things are you planning to achieve today? How many things are pulling you in different directions right now?

Would it be excellent, good, incredible to have peace of mind instead of all that commotion?

You can.

Decide right now only to have one goal, and that is to have peace of mind.

Everything else is simplified when that is the only thing you focus on.

When our goal, our aim, is peace of mind, our next step is forgiveness. Forgiving everyone and anyone who troubles us because of their behaviour, if not one of love, is a cry for help. And then, as we forgive them, we can approach them and their challenges with love.

We can have peace of mind.

When you've seen beyond yourself, then you may find, peace of mind is waiting there.

George Harrison

You'll never find peace of mind until you listen to your heart.

George Michael

August 19

Insanity

I should never be left alone with my mind for too long.

Libba Bray

The moment I'm with others, everything's okay. It's only when I'm alone that the insanity of isolation swamps my mind. It is also the insanity of unfettered truths about myself.

The moment I'm with others, the front I present to the world clicks into place, and the half-truths assert themselves. After all, I'm not going to be foolish enough to tell them what's really going on. What would they think? I have an image to maintain. I'm unsure what that image might be, but I'm not taking any risks.

And the interesting thing about all that is I don't even know what the real truths about myself are. We don't know what they are. I don't even know if they exist. They are more like a saucepan full of dark goo that nobody knows what to do with anymore.

I know the solution. Talk about it with someone. That clears it away.

I became insane with long intervals of horrible sanity.

Edgar Allan Poe

When we remember we are all mad, the mysteries disappear and life stands explained.

Mark Twain

August 20

Causes

We often tend to ignore how much of a child is still in all of us.

Elisabeth Kübler-Ross

I meet people who search throughout their lives, trying to find the reason, the deep root cause for their life's troubles.

I was curious and searched for the source of my personal insecurities and frailties.

Then I remembered. When I was eight years old, I got a part in the school play, 'Toad of Toad Hall'.

I was one of the dormouse carol singers that went to Badger's home. Badger wasn't there, but Ratty and Mole were in. I had a line explaining how wonderful Badger had been when he was there. The line was, 'And once he gave us steak and kidney pudding!'

I learnt my line. I knew it. Then the director said that I was putting the emphasis on the wrong word. So he took my line away and gave it to someone else.

That's it! That's why I've been doomed to fail all my life!

(Emoji weeping face)

And the worst thing is that I still have no idea which word should have the emphasis.

Is it – **And** once he gave us steak and kidney pudding or – And **once** he gave, or – And once he **gave** us, or – And once he gave us **steak** and kidney, or – And once he gave us steak **and** kidney......

Help me, please. Tell me the truth. Which should it be? Allow me to find peace in this world, in my life.

I have since identified one or two other things that may have contributed to the troubles in my life. Thank God!

In every real man a child is hidden that wants to play.

Friedrich Nietzsche

August 21

Ego

I look both ways before I cross a one-way street. That's how little faith I have left in humanity.

Jack Nicholson

I know the voices aren't real, but man, do they ever come up with some great ideas.

Jack Nicholson

Oh, how we want to do some of those things, we know we shouldn't. Oh, how the temptation grows and bubbles up inside us.

'No! No!' We cry. And try to change the subject.

'Isn't it a beautiful day? So many exciting things I could do...' But somehow, that thought still invades our mind.

Take action. Distract yourself. Do something else. Clean your shoes. Meditate, breathe.

Put a date in your diary when you can do it if you still want to.

Get busy.

List and feel gratitude for all the good things in your life. The vital word in that sentence is 'feel.' 'Feel' gratitude. Do it with your body. Do it with your soul.

Enjoy your life.

I don't care what you all think about me. I don't think about you at all.

Jack Nicholson

Sometimes I look at people and think, 'Really? That's the sperm that won?'

Jack Nicholson

August 22

Peace

Nothing good ever comes of violence.

Martin Luther King Jnr

An eye for an eye will only make the whole world blind.

Mahatma Gandhi

The world is suffering from an epidemic of fear and aggression. It is contagious. And actually, this illness has been raging across the world for millennia. It isn't easy to imagine a world where this is not the case.

And what good would it do if you and I stopped engaging in it? Wouldn't we be taken advantage of, overwhelmed, and trampled by the endless stream of attacks?

But everything changes by shedding my desire to attack, discarding my attack thoughts, and replacing them with love. Any negative thought, word or action is an attack thought. And behind any of those is a desire, a crying out for love, a want to be loved and feel secure.

So when we replace our attack thoughts with love and peace, we allow their desire for love and peace to grow.

There are many people who feel that it is useless and futile to continue talking about peace and non-violence against a government whose only reply is savage attacks on an unarmed and defenceless people.

Nelson Mandela

Thoughts

We are shaped by our thoughts, we become what we think. When the mind is pure, joy follows like a shadow that never leaves.

Buddha

The average person (who is average?) has between 12,000 and 60,000 thoughts per day. Of those, 80% are negative and harmful, and 95% repeat yesterday's thoughts.

Makes you think, eh?

Makes me watchful?

It makes me more careful about what I let in.

Any negative input breeds more negativity.

If we don't watch, read, or listen to more of the news than we have to. If we don't deluge ourselves with all the negative stuff in soaps, hospital programs and gossip, we have a chance of shedding negativity.

There are amazing, uplifting books we can listen to or read.

Oh yes, and we can meditate.

Let's guard our minds and choose what we feed them,

You are more than your thoughts, your body or your feelings. You are a swirling vortex of limitless potential who is here to shake things up and create something new that the universe has never seen.

Dr Richard Bartlett

Mistakes

A mistake will work out to your advantage.

Chinese fortune cookie

That's what I got in my fortune cookie the other day as I finished my meal with my son.

It is such a relief to realise that. It means – it seems to me – that there are no mistakes.

There are no mistakes because everything we do is a learning process we are here to experience.

The important thing, of course, is to learn from the things that we do. If we repeat them, they are no longer mistakes. They are defiant acts of stupidity.

We want to grow. We want to learn how to live the life we inhabit.

If we are still doing things because of the expectations our mothers had when we were kids, that truly is a mistake. It is time to grow up, discard our idiotic behaviours and start to live.

Cut your apron strings and grow up.

Nothing wise was ever printed on an apron.

Demetri Martin

Kids are supposed to grow up and cut the apron strings. I just never dreamed those sharp scissors would leave so many wounds.

Lisa Wingate

Behaviour

We ourselves feel that what we are doing is just a drop in the ocean. But if that drop was not in the ocean, I think the ocean would be less because of that missing drop. I do not agree with the big way of doing things. To us what matters is the individual.

Mother Teresa

It is so easy to ignore or belittle what we do. To think that it makes no difference.

While in fact, everything we do impacts everything and everyone. No one and nothing can fill our space. We are part of the whole.

If we were not here, doing, then it would be as if someone had removed a thread from a stunningly beautiful tapestry. Not good.

So have the courage and the insight to recognise your importance. And do your best to do your best and make a positive difference everywhere you go.

Have fun with it. Pat yourself on your back. Indulge. Enjoy.

The things that are most important don't always scream the loudest.

Bob Hawke

Whatever you do will be insignificant, but it is very important that you do it.

Mahatma Gandhi

Living

Get involved. You don't want to look back on your life and realise that you successfully managed to stay out of it.

Robert Breault

Don't be withdrawn. Don't hide yourself away. Exist in the world you live in, it needs you. It is expecting you. It is counting on you. And you are relying on it.

You can almost hear the heavy metal doors clanging shut when you isolate!

We were put on the earth to interact with others. When we don't, each time we don't, we are taking our piece out of their jigsaw puzzle and flicking it into a corner of the room.

And the things we do or do not do today are the seeds of our future. People need people. When we fall, we need a hand to help us up. The more hands, the better.

We want to interact with others. We want to listen to and help others. We want to live our lives in this world. We do not want it to happen without us.

We don't function well as human beings when we are in isolation.

Robert Zemeckis

No man is an island, entire of itself.

John Donne

August 27

Worry

Worry does not empty tomorrow of its sorrow, it empties today of its strength.

Corrie Ten Boom

Worry is mental toilet cleaner, eating away at 99.9% of all known peace!

And on top of which, (if that's not bad enough) our unconscious and the universe does its best to create what we think and focus on.

Perhaps the good thing (maybe not) is that our worry is often not even specific. We fill our mind and body with the dis-ease, the feeling of dread. We allow it to permeate our being without even considering what we are worrying about.

And it is all the handiwork of our old friend(!?), the ego.

As soon as we discard the ego's insanity and access our inner peace, the worry disappears. It is that simple. We just have to do it.

If a problem is fixable, if a situation is such that you can do something about it, then there is no need to worry. If it's not fixable, then there is no help in worrying. There is no benefit to worrying whatsoever.

Dalai Lama

August 28

Tiredness

*The most critical time in any battle is not when I'm
fatigued, it's when I no longer care.*

Craig D Lounsbrough

Very occasionally, I wake up feeling tired. My body
sluggish, my mind in a mud hole, just a pathetic head and
hand sticking out, too blah even to wave.

When I do not feel like that and read the above, I think
it's never that bad!

And yet, when it is not good, my first thought is to attack
myself for being a failure or useless.

But if it is happening, it is there for a reason. Something
mental or physical is waving to me. It is asking for help.

So, the very least I can do is be tolerant and loving
towards myself. To welcome myself slowly and kindly back
into the world of action.

And it also makes sense to ponder on its causes. To look
at what is going on in my life, physically and mentally, that
could be the cause of this lethargy and, where possible, begin
to make the necessary changes.

*'I must be overtired,' Buttercup managed. 'The excitement
and all.'*
*'Rest then', her mother cautioned. 'Terrible things can
happen when you're overtired. I was overtired the night
your father proposed!'*

William Goldman

August 29

Behaviour

I shall look at you out of the corner of my eye, and you will say nothing. Words are the source of misunderstandings.

Antione de Saint-Exupéry

When I sit by my window looking over the river in the morning, my dog curls up on my feet as I read and meditate.

Is it because of the peace I am in?

Then, when I move over to this table to sit and write, she often gets up onto my lap. She wants to be involved, poking my pens and paper with her nose.

We are giving off information to the people we are with all the time, whether we are speaking or not.

So if we communicate with a gentle feeling of love and quiet, they will know this at some level and be far more open.

The way we communicate with others and with ourselves ultimately determines the quality of our lives.

Tony Robbins

August 30

Drink

First, you take a drink, then the drink takes a drink, then the drink takes you.

F Scott Fitzgerald

Your addiction is not you, but it feels like you because you've spent so much intimate time together.

Toni Sorenson

When I tell people I have not had a drink for 40 years, they say things like, 'Well done,' with probably a gosh or two thrown in.

But is it not well done. Maybe it was well done for the first year or so, but then, as I began to tread a spiritual path, 'well done' no longer came into it.

Every so often, my ego tells me lies about how good it would be to have a drink, but I know they are lies. I know where the drink led me. I remember the bottomless pit of despair and self-hatred that comes with a drink.

And why on earth would I want to go back to that?

That is all I need to remember.

Every experience in your life is being orchestrated to teach you something you need to know to move forward.

Brian Tracy

What progress, you ask, have I made? I have begun to be a friend to myself.

Hecato of Rhodes

August 31

Mistakes

If you fail to plan, you are planning to fail.

Benjamin Franklin

The time to repair the roof is when the sun is shining.

John F Kennedy

Many people berate themselves when they fail. They relive the failure over and over again.

There is no such thing as failure. What we have is feedback on what we did. We can look at the event, take the feedback, learn from it, and plan how to do things differently next time.

And even if you will never be able to repeat the event, there are things that you can learn from your feedback that you can apply to other areas of your life.

So even if you didn't win a gold medal in the Olympics, and you will never be able to compete again, you have feedback that you can use throughout your life.

Enjoy.

The future is already here – it's just not evenly distributed.

William Gibson

Someone is sitting in the shade today because someone planted a tree a long time ago.

Warren Buffett

We only

achieve

by doing

September 1

Visualising

To accomplish great things, we must first dream, then visualise, then plan... believe... act!

Alfred A Montapert

Successful athletes visualise themselves achieving and succeeding at what they do brilliantly. They take time to imagine themselves, making the catch, hitting the winning ball, etc. They are good at what they do. One of the reasons they are good is because they use visualisation to cement their achievements into their being.

They go to the end of the event in their minds and live the success that comes with achieving what they want.

It would surely make sense for us to do the same for our upcoming tasks. Even if all we have to look forward to is another day at the office or tidying the house after the whirlwind of other humans have left.

If we take a little time to visualise it all going supremely well, it will be much better than we might otherwise expect.

Make sure you visualise what you really want, not what someone else wants for you.

Jerry Gillies

September 2

Breathing

Sometimes, the most important thing in a whole day is the rest we take between two deep breaths.

Etty Hillesum

That is a pretty profound statement, isn't it?

The rest between two deep breaths, and if that is the most important thing, that changes the perspective on everything else.

On all the things we dash through the day trying to accomplish.

More deep breaths, then...

Lots more.

Take a deep breath and pause for one minute without doing anything! There did you feel the magic?

Avijeet Das

September 3

Love

Those who love deeply never grow old; they may die of old age, but they die young.

Benjamin Franklin

I just watched a couple in their 60s walking their dog. They were holding hands. It was so beautiful. It's so wonderful to see love and oneness together.

How magical to have someone's hand to hold. To be chosen.

May you delight in such gentle intimacy, too.

You are my heart, my life, my one and only thought.

Arthur Conan Doyle

Rejection

The fear of rejection is worse than rejection itself.

Nora Profit

Fear of rejection.

Although we probably don't verbalise it like that. We go through our day, our lives with a mental hand reaching out in front of us, exploring the world. Like a child in a dark room, its arms outstretched as it creeps across the unknown floor.

Fear of rejection. Fear that if we offer love, affection and friendship, it won't be accepted.

Maybe recognising this will make us less vulnerable.

We know what we give to the world, we get back. So, it makes much more sense to give the world love, affection and friendship.

If you stop being afraid of the word no and take more chances, you will get more yes.

Jeanette Coron

Every time I thought I was being rejected from something good, I was actually being redirected to something better.

Steve Maraboli

Doing Good

Apathy is a trap. There is no challenge... so there is no reward. Remember, there is always free cheese in a mouse trap.

Steve Maraboli

Hey. Do you want a reward today, a present, a little parcel of joy?

Easy.

Do something for someone else. Reach out and touch their life.

We tend to think of ourselves as separate. All individual beings doing our best to enjoy, get along with, or put up with others.

We are mistaken. We are all one entity. One collective, all on the same journey together.

So every time we do something, in fact, anything, for someone else, we are benefitting ourselves too.

It doesn't mean that everyone else will treat us well. But by giving out love, we are opening ourselves to love.

We can remember that everyone suffers from fear when we are greeted with hostility. And helping anyone is such a good thing to be doing.

Dogs and philosophers do the greatest good and get the fewest rewards.

Diogenes

Knowledge

The more I read, the more I acquire, the more certain I am that I know nothing.

Voltaire

I don't know.

Sometimes, maybe even often, I like to think that I do know, but I suspect that is an illusion.

Yes, there are things that I do know, but are they the things that matter?

Sometimes, when I am with people, I know that I say the right thing, and when that happens, I know what I am saying does not come from me.

Yes, I'd like to claim it. I want to be wise and able to shower people with enlightenment, but if I am honest, I know that I cannot.

All I can do is be a channel for them whenever possible. There are times when I do not know what to say or think. When that happens, it is easier for me to say, 'I don't know'.

Admitting that I don't know the answer makes it easier for me to travel through my day, being there for myself and others, witnessing life as it unfolds.

It is easier to make decisions because I am no longer trying to control everything.

Knowing yourself is the beginning of all wisdom.

Carl Jung

September 7

New Day

Don't limit yourself based only on what you see in front of you today. You have the potential to turn it around.

Germany Kent

It's a new dawn
It's a new day
It's a new life for me
And I'm feeling good.

Leslie Bricusse

It's a new day.

Today is new.

It can be as new as we choose to make it.

We can allow the newness of today to permeate all areas of our lives. We can go through today like a young child discovering the world for the first time and opening up all our senses (both mental and physical) sight, touch, taste, sound, and smell. We can embrace the fullness of it all. Consuming every experience slowly and eagerly, noticing everything as if for the first time.

We can have courage. We can dare to make a decision we have been delaying. We already know what we are going to do, so why wait any longer? It's a new day. A new life. Let us be brave and live it fully.

Isn't it nice to think that tomorrow is a new day with no mistakes in it yet?

L M Montgomery

Life always offers you a second chance. It's called tomorrow.

Stephen King

September 8

Motivation

Only I can change my life. No one can do it for me.

Carol Burnett

We are motivated in two ways, 'away' from things or 'toward' things.

An away-from graph looks like a range of mountain peaks and valleys. Let's look at a graph about our money.

We have to pay rent, or you need money for a holiday. We are seriously motivated to get the money. (If we don't, we'll have nowhere to live.) So we put all our energy and focus into getting the money.

But the motivation goes when we've paid the rent, so we relax until the next demand.

A toward graph is a line going up and up as we move towards our goal. We want to sail around the world. We earn some money, buy a rope, then a sail, put a deposit on a boat, then a sleeping bag. Everything we do moves us closer to having the boat and setting off.

Away motivation has serious intensity, no money, no house.

Toward motivation is much more measured. And the goal is constantly drawing us onward.

We want to have toward motivation, it accomplishes things, it feels good, and we don't burn out.

Life is 10% what happens to you and 90% how you react to it.

Charles R Swindoll

September 9

Namaste

Namaste. It was a Nepalese greeting. It meant: The light within me bows to the light within you.

Jennifer Donnelly

Namaste.

A gentle greeting.

For a while, I met and heard people using it with no idea of its meaning.

Should I be using it?

Then, one day, I read: 'The spirit in me bows to the spirit in you'.

I thought, wow, that's the greeting I want to use. So, I'm gently pushing it out into the world.

With quiet love.

Namaste, a person says, and with just one word, she acknowledges so much. She acknowledges the existence of the soul, she acknowledges the existence of the soul within her, she acknowledges the existence of the soul within other people, and she acknowledges the need to remember this holiest of holy truths often.

Sean Patrick Brennan

September 10

Surrender

Letting go. Everyone talks about it like it's the easiest thing.
Uncurl your fingers one by one until your hand is open. But
my hand has been clenched into a fist for three years now;
it's frozen shut.

Gayle Forman

When we have a challenge, a problem, call it what you will, our natural reaction is to dive into it. To try to solve it. To become completely immersed in it.

And often, that only leads to us being part of the problem. We may even start to shout abuse silently or aloud at ourselves or those involved.

Here's a thought. When was the last time you had a challenge and someone shouted like a sergeant-major at you? Telling you how incompetent you were, that a half-wit like you should not be allowed out of the house, they've met donkeys with more intellect than you. (Sure, those are all the wrong examples, so make up or remember some of your own.)

What I was wondering was, did being shouted at help?

Did you suddenly see what needed doing with exceptional clarity?

Thinking it to yourself has the same effect as being told it by someone else.

Instead, let go. Surrender. Step back mentally and physically and wait for the answer.

It will come.

Who looks outside, dreams; who looks inside, awakens.

Carl Jung

September 11

Resentments

As smoking is to the lungs, so is resentment to the soul; even one puff is bad for you.

Elizabeth Gilbert

Our resentments go out into the ether. They are not something that only affects us. It is worse than that. They go out from us and affect the people we are with.

A poisonous gas pervading the space that we occupy.

Yes, the resentments certainly damage us with their poison. They belittle us. They eat away at our souls.

They are the destructive fuels that our ego uses to control and diminish us. All of which is reason enough for any sane person to discard them.

Let go of resentments. They do not reward us in the way we've been tricked into believing.

Our fatigue is often caused not by work, but by worry frustration and resentment.

Dale Carnegie

I started to realise how the conditions of our hearts affects the way we see. If your heart is full of bitterness, anger and resentment, you're going to look at the world as a very evil place.

Danny Gokey

September 12

Stupidity

Only two things are infinite, the universe and stupidity, and I'm not sure about the former.

Albert Einstein

Ah, Stupidity.

I googled stupidity and found a neon sign, 'NO STUPID PEOPLE BEYOND THIS POINT.' Interestingly, the D in STUPID was not lit.

How many people do you think the sign stops?

One of the most dangerous things about stupidity is that the stupid person does not know they are stupid.

Only a truly stupid person would think that they are never stupid. Which is a relief for me, as it makes accepting my moments of stupidity easier to bear. But the trouble with stupidity is that it is dangerous. We do dangerous or potentially dangerous things when we are being stupid.

We say yes to things we don't want to do when we are being stupid. And even if the thing itself is not dangerous, it is still dangerous to us. Mentally, at the very least, because it damages our self-esteem and inner being. We think less of ourselves.

So, while we will continue to be stupid, perhaps, now warned, we can do it less often.

Stupidity is far more dangerous than evil, for evil takes a break from time to time, stupidity does not.

Anatole France

Think how stupid the average person is, and realise half of them are stupider than that.

George Carlin

September 13

Change

Putting people DOWN does not make you a powerful and strong person – it makes you a bully, a coward, and eventually alone in life.

Tess Calomino

Sometimes, we put up with stuff for too long. We go along with what 'they' want, or perhaps what we think they want, without ever talking about it.

We get locked into it and don't dare to suggest, question, or discuss it with anyone.

And yet, when you think about it logically, what's the worst thing they can say, 'No. That's the way it is. Put up with it.'

(They may not use those words. They may want to dress it up a little to appear better.) But if they do say, 'No', we are no worse off than we are now.

And much more often than not, if we question how things are and ask for change, they will meet us halfway.

(We may revert to things being the way they were. We're used to that. So you question it again.)

Go on. Be brave. Live.

The worst that can happen is they say, 'No'.

There is a stubbornness about me that never can bear to be frightened at the will of others. My courage always rises at every attempt to intimidate me.

Jane Austin

Self-Love

If we want to fully experience love and belonging we must believe we are worthy of love and belonging.

Brené Brown

Which of these is the most important for you?

To be able to love.

To be loved.

To realise that you deserve to be loved.

The most important (although we may not have considered it) is to realise that we deserve to be loved.

Loving and being loved for most of us is easy to a greater or lesser extent.

But the very idea that we deserve to be loved... is something else altogether.

It is so easy to push our 'worthiness' down. To judge ourselves as failures in one way or another.

You can search the entire universe and not find a single being more worthy of love than you.

Buddha

And too often, we forget that we're worthy of our own love too.

Dhiman

September 15

Past

Even God cannot change the past.

Agathon

Nothing can be done about it, except go to the memory and make ourselves miserable. So why are we beating ourselves up about it?

All we have is now.

Here, now, is where we can make a difference. Or not. But nowhere else.

Discard misery and guilt and make changes to who we are today.

Be alive.

Live.

Embrace the opportunities we are offered.

If you can't change it... change the way you think about it.

Mary Engelbreit

Attention

I give everywhere I go, even if only a smile, a compliment or my full attention. Listening is the best gift I can give to those around me.

Jonathan Lehmann

Full Attention.

So important.

I was at the self-checkout, scanning and bagging my shopping, and I chatted to the lady watching the checkouts.

I asked about her Christmas, but I didn't hear, take in, her reply. But I got a notion that it had not been the best. So when I had finished packing, I turned and gave her my full attention.

'I'm sorry, I didn't take all that in properly. What happened?'

Apparently, her husband of thirty years had up and left her just before Christmas. So she had been alone on Christmas Day.

All of which was, I guess, a gentle nudge from the universe to remind me to listen properly.

I'm so glad I didn't just say, 'That was nice, happy new year.' That would have been a major 'oops'.

People will reveal who they are if you just pay attention.

Germany Kent

September 17

Now

The only impossible journey is the one you never begin.

Tony Robbins

This moment is precious.

So very precious. You will never have it again.

There it is gone. Gone forever.

It's so easy to squander them without even bothering to notice them.

It is so magical and enriching to notice them. To actually take in what is happening. To honestly engage with the world that is presenting itself to us. And use our senses fully.

Acknowledge, go into, and experience what we are feeling, seeing, tasting, touching, hearing.

Be alive.

Live.

Savour.

Enjoy.

True happiness is… to enjoy the present without anxious dependence upon the future.

Seneca

September 18

Self-Care

The morning sun is out and bright. Forcing night to sneak away without a fight.

Richard L Ratliff

The days are getting shorter, affecting us, even if we do not realise it. We thrive in the light. It feeds and stimulates us.

So when the days shorten, part of our being starts to withdraw, to begin to hide.

Therefore, it is essential to ensure that we immerse ourselves in whatever light there is at some point in the day. To consciously allow the light to flow into us and fill us.

It does not need to be long. Just long enough to stop the decay from setting in. Charging us so that we can reach the next day, still shining.

Happiness often sneaks in through a door you didn't know you left open

John Barrymore

Sunbeams everywhere and mist floating, like freshly minted souls.

Haruki Murakami

Self-love

I love myself unconditionally, as it is essential to my happiness. I love the person that I am, and I do not need other people's approval to love myself fully.

Jonathon Lehmann

That pretty much says it all, doesn't it?
It is something to aspire to achieve.
Are you loving yourself unconditionally?
Do you love the person you are without others' approval?
Maybe it helps to realise that others find this a challenge.

I have come to believe that caring for myself is not self-indulgent. Caring for myself is an act of survival.

Audre Lorde

September 20

Anger

Whatever is begun in anger ends in shame.

Benjamin Franklin

Anger!

That moment when we lash out in rage. Or perhaps even worse, the internal bubbling of anger or discontent. Forever simmering inside us, waiting to erupt and waiting for the right moment to lash out and defend ourselves with attack.

But when we peel away the layers, it covers fear and sadness and our need to hide.

Discard anger and sadness floods through us.

Look deeply into the sadness, and you will find, at its core, fear.

If we dare to delve into its source, we'll see the futility of it. It is possible to push the fear aside. It is, after all, a lie.

We can discard anger. We can choose peace. But first, we have to dislodge the lie that is our fear.

Yes, it is possible to do this. But simply reading this without internal thought and action will achieve – nothing.

There are two things that a person should never be angry at, what they can help and what they cannot.

Plato

Cause

Silence and invisibility go hand in hand with powerlessness.

Audre Lorde

If we want to change, 'get better', and have more comfort or peace in our lives, it will not happen by simply clapping our hands and expecting transformation.

Often, people experience dis-quiet, dis-ease, dis-harmony in their lives but never peel back the layers far enough to uncover the root cause.

And we are trained to deal with the symptoms, not the cause. Got a headache? Take a tablet. Feel depressed? Take a tablet.

In the twelve-step recovery programs, the first step they take is 'Admitted they are powerless over "the cause" and that their lives have become unmanageable'.

It is a good starting point to recognise and accept the cause. Once we have identified it and accepted our powerlessness over it, we are possibly ready to start the journey to change.

It always seems impossible until it's done.

Nelson Mandela

Happiness is not something you postpone for the future; it is something you design for the present.

Jim Rohn

Life

This is my simple religion. There is no need for temples, no need for complicated philosophy. Our own brain, our own heart is our temple; the philosophy is kindness.

Dalai Lama

Life is complicated. A struggle. We are swept back and forth by the tide as it rises and falls.

We crave order and peace. We desire success, friendship and love.

To achieve any of this, we want calm and quiet.

Little moments of peace that can spread into the rest of our day.

Meditation and reflection.

Life is really simple, but we insist on making it complicated.

Confucius

Behaviour

If you want to change attitudes, start with a change in behaviour.

William Glasser

Don't let the behaviour or misbehaviour of others have control over you.

Don't let other people's rudeness, anger, disrespect, or lack of consideration affect you.

You have a choice over how you react, feel, behave, think.

You have control over yourself. Provided you choose to exercise it.

And yes, you can.

Yes, I'm still going to misbehave.

Amy Winehouse

Your nerve coatings are only so thick. When they get worn really thin and frayed, that's when people say things, do things, misbehave.

Don Felder

September 24

Self-Love

It's amazing how words can do that – just shred your insides apart.

Lauren Oliver

What do you think about yourself?

What do you say to yourself?

What would you do if you had a neighbour who said those things to you? Stop talking to them, I suspect. I know I would.

I discovered that I had a choice. I discovered that it is possible not to put myself down or belittle myself.

Most of the time, I choose to say positive, uplifting, supportive, and loving things to myself. And I prefer life when I'm doing that.

I can feel at ease. I go into my mind, and it says, 'You're doing well. Keep it up. Enjoy.' So I do.

I know that the negative thoughts and words are still there, hovering, waiting for their chance, but I leave them alone and get on with having a peaceful time.

Sticks and stones may break my bones, but words... they'll destroy me.

Cassandra Giovanni

It only takes a second to call a girl fat, and she'll take a lifetime trying to starve herself.

Harry Styles

September 25

Patience

Patience is the road to wisdom.

Kao Kalia Yang

There are days, mornings usually, when I sit down and write two or possibly three of these writings, one after another. They pour out of my pen and onto the page.

Then, there are days when there is nothing. And if that continues for a few days, I start to fear. Will I ever write again? Has it ended?

I forget that it has always been like this.

And I think there are many areas in our lives when we get caught in their highs and lows.

Allowing fear in.

So important to remember and know that everything changes all the time. And it's okay.

Better to relax and wait with faith than to do fear. Much better.

If there is one thing that has made a difference in my life, it is the courage to turn and face what wants to change within me.

Elizabeth Lesser

September 26

Self-Love

Your need for acceptance can make you invisible in this world. Don't let anything stand in the way of the light that shines through this form. Risk being seen in all of your glory.

Jim Carrey

You were somebody before you accepted the role you identify with. And you were somebody else before that too.

So, think back in silence, just enquiring, who am I? Who was I?

And before that.

And before that.

Peel away the layers.

Find yourself.

And consider how much of that is reflected now. Have you lost more than you have gained by becoming today's model?

Are there aspects of yourself you want to reawaken and love now?

Explore.

Enjoy.

The darkness makes everything disappear, but it makes nothing go away.

Craig D Lounsbrough

Action

Everything I say and do is connected to my happiness and my ability to love.

Jonathan Lehmann

Everything.
Everything I say and do.
Everything.
It makes one think, does it not?
It makes one want to proceed with caution. To take care of what one does and says.

When you have once seen the glow of happiness on the face of a beloved person, you know that a man can have no vocation but to awaken that light on the faces surrounding him. In the depth of winter, I finally learned that within me there lay an invisible summer.

Albert Camus

September 28

Ego

*The ego says, 'I shouldn't have to suffer,' and that thought
makes you suffer so much more. It is a distortion of the
truth, which is always paradoxical. The truth is that you
need to say yes to suffering before you can transcend it.*

Eckhart Tolle

How we fight suffering, not realising that we are
only strengthening it, making it worse, extending its
life.

The way to move on from it is to accept that it exists.

When we can realise that what we are going through
is just what we are going through, we can begin to find
release.

We can move towards freedom.

The ego is sustained through conscious resistance.

Eckhart Tolle

September 29

Being

Challenges are meant to be met and overcome.

Liu Xiang

We're not meant to be perfect. It took me a long time to learn that.

Jane Fonda

I'm a big believer in everything is meant to be. If it didn't work out then, it's fine.

Amine

You are, right now, exactly where you are meant to be, and everything you are going through is exactly as it is supposed to be.

Here's the thing, whether you believe that or not, accept for a moment that it is true.

Accepting it suddenly releases all of the pressure from your life.

If what is happening now, or in three days, is what is meant, then...

It does not mean we stop doing our best in the current situation. It means the outcome will be the outcome that is intended to happen.

We can enjoy the present moment as much as is possible because all those self-imposed pressures no longer exist.

Sometimes, it takes a wrong turn to get you to the right place.

Mandy Hale

September 30

Inner Voice

*When we direct a lot of hostile energy towards the inner
critic, we enter into a losing battle.*

Sharon Salzberg

Even when we are meditating, reading, relaxing, letting go, our ego is there, yakking away in the background.

Judging, poking, belittling, putting down, or even just chattering on about any old rubbish it can to distract us.

And that's on a good day when things are going well.

God help us when things are going badly.

We can (we probably won't, certainly won't if the ego can stop us) go into the peace inside us. Into the light and the calm. The ego cannot enter.

We can empower ourselves, and the ego's rubbish will bounce off us, like water off a windscreen.

For a while, anyway.

We can do that if we choose.

We can.

Trust your Inner-Creator and let go of your inner-critic.

J R Incer

I am

responsible

October 1

Emptiness

She was tired, with that tiredness that only emptiness brings.

Paolo Giordano

The greatest tragedies in life is not an untimely death, but to live a life of emptiness.

Topsy Gift

Sometimes, a wave of emptiness, blackness, or perhaps darkness flutters over and through us. A little cloud of disease wraps itself around us. Maybe a shadow of loneliness and self-pity gently puts its arm around our shoulders.

And we can, of course, go down with it at that moment and amuse ourselves by becoming totally immersed in 'the awfulness' of it all.

However, if we don't want to do that, one of the best things we can do is to get up and move around. Move.

The next thing to do is to think about others. Who can you call? Not to complain to but to find out with love and interest how they are doing. Shift your focus. Speaking to people is so much better than texting. When we text, we edit and therefore lie.

Go out for a walk, if possible, among people. See how many smiles you can get. Can you make someone laugh? Tell someone why you've come out on your walk.

Be honest.

Be free.

The inner emptiness is the door to God.

Swami Dhyan Giten

October 2

Homelessness

People who are homeless are not social inadequates. They are people without homes.

Sheila McKechnie

If you see someone sitting by the road, don't just put money in their cup. Talk to them. Have a conversation with them. Please find out about them. Not many people are interested in them. Change their day by treating them as a human.

Do it on days you feel good and when you don't.

Words and kindness mean so much more to people with struggles than a hastily thrown coin.

We have come dangerously close to accepting the homeless situation as a problem that we just can't solve.

Linda Lingle

October 3

Tranquility

*It is in your power to withdraw yourself whenever you
desire. Perfect tranquility within consists in the good
ordering of the mind, the realm of your own.*

Marcus Aurelius

Tranquility.

The word comes from the Latin 'trans', meaning
exceedingly and 'quies', meaning quiet or rest.

Exceedingly quiet.

Wow.

And you have done it. Go back to a time when you felt
tranquil. (If you really cannot think of one, then bring to
mind someone you know who has tranquility. And think of a
time when you've seen them being tranquil.)

So go to that time of tranquility and create that feeling in
your body. Make it bigger and stronger so it flows through
you.

Move the feeling into your heart and embrace the sense of
peace.

Breathe in and out slowly.

Let the wonder of tranquility expand, and become aware
of the ease within your mind.

Breathe in and out before you start anything for the rest
of your day or your life if you're sensible. Before you answer
your phone, before you drive off, before you get up in the
morning before you choose anything.

Transform your life and yourself with exceeding peace.

*The more tranquil a man becomes, the greater is his
success, his influence, his power for good. Calmness of mind
is one of the beautiful jewels of wisdom.*

James Allen

October 4

Equality

This is a man's world
But it wouldn't be nothing
Nothing without a woman or a girl.

James Brown

The inequality and disrespect for women, prevalent amongst men, makes me want to throw up.

There, I've said it. The whole attitude is that it's a woman's job to clean and tidy, cook or wash.

The snide sexist jokes and put-downs that go by unchallenged.

If you are in a group of men and one of them says sexist things, you are part of it if you do not challenge it.

It will only change and cease if we dare to act.

Not acting is endorsing the whole attitude.

Ignoring a child's disrespect is the surest guarantee that it will continue.

Fred G Gosman

October 5

Self-Torture

Before you accuse me, take a look at yourself.

Ellas McDaniel

It is so easy to blame others, to dissect their faults, without glancing at ours.

One of the extreme and obvious cases of this is when couples separate. We ignore the idea that we could possibly be at fault for any of it.

We only focus on the other's shortcomings, discarding all the good things they may have done.

We turn everything they do into an attack. We allow the hatred to seethe through us, blinding us in our dealings with 'them' and every area of our lives.

And interestingly, it does not add to the likelihood that we will 'win'.

We are poisoned.

Poisoned by ourselves. They have not poisoned us.

It's such a strange thing to choose to do.

Self-harm – the world will come at you with knives anyway. You do not need to beat them to it.

Caitlin Moran

October 6

Denial

We are often tempted to make all our troubles big, bigger, biggest.

Swimming through the mud as we cry out, 'I would change direction, but I've got mud in my eyes. I am hopeless and helpless. And anyway, it is all 'their' fault'.

Such nonsense, such a stupid lie. We shout it out because we need to tell everyone and drag them down to our level so that they can strengthen our belief.

I'm okay as long as it is all 'their fault'. I am doing 'all' I can. I am 'wallowing.' Surely, I should be allowed to 'wallow'. It is, after all, all 'their fault'.

And as long as I believe that, it prevents any possibility of meaningful change. Or growth in me.

Please mark my headstone when I die with, 'It was all their fault'.

Then I shall be happy.

If you are not taking responsibility for your state of consciousness, you are not taking responsibility for life.

Eckhart Tolle

Your life begins to change the day you take responsibility for it.

Steve Maraboli

October 7

Focus

The secret of manifestation is to focus on what you want,
not on what you don't want.

Stuart Wilde

The message in that quote is so obvious.

Surely, only a lunatic would do anything different.

And yet... talking to others, it would seem that so many spend their time talking about what they do not want, over and over again.

Or focusing on the things in their past that they consider 'bad'.

They must all be indulging in insanity.

I guess they must love the pain that goes with it and be addicted to that pain. Very strange.

You are the master of your own reality. If you want to
change it, change the way you think.

Stuart Wilde

Challenges

Many rivers to cross
And it's only my will that keeps me alive.

Jimmy Cliff

There is something deep within me that keeps me going. It keeps me journeying on, regardless of the challenges I face.

And interestingly, it is the challenges that inspire me. Not perhaps, when I am in deep struggle, yet as I write that, I realise it is the challenges I enjoy.

I love being alive. I love winning my battles, especially when I am my foe!

It took me a long time to realise how wonderful difficulties are. But now I do.

In the past, someone told me to thank the difficulties, and I told him where he could go!

But now I do thank them and him. (Although I'd be quite happier if some were a little easier.)

Neither the stone that made you stumble is your enemy, nor the stone that helped you cross the river is your friend!
Universe just lives its own life!

Mehmet Murat ildan

October 9

Learning

*I am, as I've said, merely competent. But in an age of
incompetence, that makes me extraordinary.*

Billy Joel

When we are competent at something, it is much easier to
get on and do it ourselves. There... it's done. No fuss.

But...

There is more to it than that.

If we do things for them, they are not learning how to do
things themselves. And horrifying though it may seem, we
will not be here forever. So, please, don't let us produce a
generation of incompetents.

Share knowledge.

Teach.

Of course, don't nag.

Instead, withdraw and allow them to discover why they
need to do things.

It's called sharing.

It is being in a partnership.

Living.

It is easier to do a job right than explain why you didn't.

Martin Van Buren

October 10

Stopping

To me, success and fulfilment lead in two different directions, one outwardly to the hope of glory, the other inwardly to the guarantee of peace.

Rasheed Ogunlaru

All our lives, we have been searching. Searching, searching. We have been desperately hoping for fulfilment. For oneness with ourselves.

Whether we knew it or not.

Looking for answers and wholeness. Hunting for self-acceptance.

So now is the time to STOP.

Stop searching, stop everything, stop blaming yourself, and stop feeling, in some unknown way, a failure.

It does not matter. That is not where the answer is.

The answer, truth, peace, and wholeness lie within us.

The soul must first realise that something seems to be missing before it can, one day, know that nothing was missing at all.

Donna Goddard

Seeing

If you are willing to rethink how you see, you may be surprised what comes into view.

Aaron Morris

Sitting calmly and looking around me, my ego says, 'But you can only see what is here. To suggest it's what we choose to see is all nonsense. You can't change reality. Look at it. It's solid. It cannot be anything else.'

And at one level, that is undoubtedly true.

But what we see at any given moment depends on how we are at that time.

Whether we are in fight mode or full of love, our perception changes.

We become open or closed to all manner of things.

And that is just one tiny example of how things are not locked into being how they appear.

Everything you see is merely a symbol for the things you do not see.

Seth Adam Smith

Miracles are a shift in perception.

Kenneth Kapnick

October 12

Behaviour

The frog does not drink up the pond in which he lives.

Native American Proverb Sioux

We consume abundantly and mostly without thought.
We are like a reckless teenager driving someone else's overpowered car far too fast.
It is a shame.
Perhaps we want to think about it?

We do not inherit the earth from our ancestors. We borrow it from our children.

Chief Seattle – A Squamish and Duwamish Chief

October 13

Mistakes

I make mistakes like the next man. In fact, being... forgive me... rather cleverer than most men, my mistakes tend to be correspondingly huger.

J K Rowling

We make mistakes. Yes, even you and even I make mistakes. And in truth, it is not the mistakes that matter. What matters is what we do about them afterwards.

Some of us hang on to our mistakes, failures and insanities and let them eat into our soul.

We beat ourselves with guilt and shame into the next thing we do and the next thing, and so on. Approaching the world overwhelmed with negativity.

It is far better to shake all our shame, guilt and failures away, like a dog shaking water from its back, and move on.

Everybody makes mistakes. Give yourself a break. Get on with enjoying your life. If there are ways to remedy your mistakes, do them and move on.

Live!

Be Alive.

Enjoy.

Experience is making mistakes and learning from them.

Bill Ackman

Hiding

You can't find peace by hiding from life.

Nicole Kidman

There are times in my life when I want to hide, when I don't want to get up and be involved with the world, when part of me wants to withdraw.

For a long time, as I watched you all gayly going through your lives, I thought I was the only one who wanted to hide.

But then I realised, because of the odd word here and there that you let slip out, that many, if not all of you, felt the same way.

This was a genuinely marvellous relief. I am not this solitary, ghastly failure.

Moreover, I discovered that this feeling is a creation of my ego – one of its many ways of controlling me.

And I've learnt that when I choose to look for the other, the still and quiet voice of my soul, I can discard my desire to hide.

I can live and enjoy my life.

She wore a thousand faces all to hide her own.

Atticus

It is a joy to be hidden, and a disaster not to be found.

D W Winnicott

October 15

Enjoyment

True self-care is not bath salts and chocolate cake, it's making the choice to build a life you don't need to regularly escape from.

Brianna Wiest

So easy to get caught up in our work. Tunnel vision. Grind. Grind. Grind on.

All the fun, if indeed there is any, seeping away, evaporating, like the moisture in the bottom of a shallow pond at the end of summer.

Dried up. Brittle.

And when you look at it like that... well, it isn't nice, is it. No fun anywhere.

It is so important to take breaks. To mix joy into our lives.

However important 'it' all might seem now, it will no longer matter in a little while.

We do not want to 'work'. That is what shrivelled-up 'grown-ups' do.

We want to enjoy ourselves, to enjoy what we are doing. We want to make it a game, even if it is seemingly endless repetition, and find a way to break it into chunks.

Enjoy each chunk. Reward yourself after each one. Make life fun.

Have mental freedom.

Talk to yourself like you would to someone you love.

Brené Brown

October 16

Life

Our lives are unfolding perfectly.

Karen Casey

This is hard to believe at 10 p.m. when our husband drills through a pipe on the landing floor.

Ah well.

So this is meant to be. It is all part of my journey. (And his and the kids too?)

The fact that the plumbers make it far worse when they come to repair it – well, that must also be part of my journey.

I have no idea what the lesson is. Tolerance perhaps? That however bad things are, they could be far worse. Maybe the plumber has some wisdom, some deep insight that I need to hear. (Rather doubt that.)

But it certainly could be far worse. I do not know or understand what is planned for me, but if I can accept life as it happens rather than fight it, it is better for me and everyone in it with me.

Acceptance doesn't mean resignation; it means understanding that something is what it is and that there's got to be a way through it.

Michael J Fox

October 17

Prejudice

Prejudice is a chain, it can hold you. If you prejudice, you can't move, you keep prejudice for years. Never get nowhere with that.

Bob Marley

What are you prejudiced about?

We all seem to have prejudices, but we don't think of them as that. We carry on without giving it a thought.

Perhaps we want to check?

I don't know, they are yours. Do they serve you well? Do they hold you back? Do they, in some way, stifle you?

I don't know.

Have a think and a look.

We all decry prejudice, yet are all prejudiced.

Herbert Spencer

October 18

Uniqueness

What sets you apart can sometimes feel like a burden, and it's not. And a lot of the time, it's what makes you great.

Emma Stone

You are unique. There are things that you will do during your life that no one else can do. And that no one else will do if you are not there to do them.

It is easy to forget that we are unique. That we have specific things to do that only we can do. It is so easy to think less of ourselves.

And my job today, at the moment, is to remind you of your uniqueness, of the tremendous power that only you have.

Go forth, excel and enjoy.

Who you are authentically is alright.

Laverne Cox

October 19

Population

Babies are such a nice way to start people.

Don Herold

The world population is increasing. It is going up by 150 people per minute. That is five people every two seconds.

Which is, I'm sure you will agree, not a slight increase. It makes me stop and wonder what I can do or should do about it.

Is there anything?

I suspect that overpopulation leads to war. So, I arrived at the idea that the only thing I can usefully do is to spread love and peace.

I am gently hoping that the love and peace will spread. I admit it seems unlikely to spread worldwide, but it is at least worth doing if it improves my tiny corner of the world.

Sometimes the smallest things take up the most room in your heart.

Winnie the Pooh – A A Milne

October 20

Inner Being

*Where true inner freedom is, there is God. And where God
is, there we want to be.*

Henri Nouwen

The solution to all our distress, challenges, blackness, despair, anger, and fear lies within us. That is where the answer is.

Let us also remember that all those negative emotions are different disguises that fear uses.

Also, remember that they are all the creation of our ego.

And when in full swing, your ego is the master craftsman, using every trick in the book to destroy you and prevent you from finding your higher self, your inner voice, your God within.

Take a breath and cut through all the ego's turmoil into the peace within you.

Hand over your life and thoughts. Listen. Experience the peace. Become the peace.

*We cannot make it rain, but we can see to it that the rain
falls on prepared soil.*

Henri Nouwen

Conflict

*Peace is not the absence of conflict but the ability to cope
with conflict by peaceful means.*

Ronald Reagan

Let go of your conflicts.

If that is too big an ask, let go of one of them.

Go on, you can do it.

Honestly, you can.

Oh, here's something that might help you, the person
suffering because of your conflict is you. Just let it go.

Take a breath, let go of it and feel the peace that enters
your body as you do this.

If you can have peace, it changes everything else. Like the
pebble creating ripples, that one change travels throughout
the rest of your existence.

*Conflict is the nature of the world. Comfort is the nature of
the self. Seek comfort in the conflict.*

Ravi Shankar

October 22

Passion

There is no end. There is no beginning. There is only the infinite passion of life.

Federico Fellini

Perhaps I am wrong. I hope I am wrong. But it seems that so many people do not have passion in their lives. They trudge through their days, just doing the same things repeatedly.

So here's a thought. What can you do in the next 24 hours, or if you like, the next seven days, with infinite passion?

Think.

Commit.

Do.

Repeat.

Live.

The two most important days of your life are the day you were born, and the day you find out why.

Mark Twain

Moving On

If you are focussing on falling bricks, you will never realise they are truly stepping stones you need to cross over to the next phase of your life.

Kemi Sogunle

Our problems exist in their current form because we have accepted them in that way with our mind.

Our ego wants us to have problems and to suffer. And so we see the issue through the ego's eyes.

But if we change how we look at them, they change.

The moment we view them through the eyes of our inner being, they change.

And we can do that with every challenge and problem we have whenever we choose to. And given how much easier, simpler, and more manageable our challenges are when we do that, why would we ever decide not to?

Oh yes, of course, our ego... But it is not actually in charge unless we allow it to be.

The mirror is where you find a reflection of your appearance. The heart is where you find a reflection of the soul.

Linda Armstrong

October 24

Yet

*What a wonderful thought it is that some of the best days of
our lives haven't even happened yet.*

Anne Frank

'Yet' is such a powerful word.

Do you use it?

People say, 'I can't do that.'

If you say to them, 'You can't do that <u>yet</u>', it changes it for them.

It opens the gate of possibility. There is light somewhere ahead.

If you ever say to yourself – 'I can't do it.' Change that, please, to, 'I can't do that <u>yet</u>.'

So different.

*If you lost it, it's because you're meant to find something
better. Trust, let go, and make room for what's coming.*

Mandy Hale

October 25

Equality

If all men are born free, how is it that all women are born slaves?

Mary Astell

How worrying. How utterly horrifying and shameful. I'm a man, and the axe I am sharpening is mine.

One of our problems is that we are programmed from birth into our roles and behaviours. So, how we behave today is inherited.

And today, it is a total nonsense.

Why should he lounge on the sofa while she cooks, cleans, washes, and has a job?

Please don't do it.

If they don't load the dishwasher, serve their next meal on a dirty plate. If they leave their clothes on the floor, throw them away. They can iron their clothes whilst they're watching TV. They are not the master. No one has that right.

Tell them that just because you want a cuddle on the sofa, it doesn't necessarily mean you want to make love.

If you don't want to make love, don't do it.

We are all humans. Let us treat each other like humans.

As equals.

Equality is the soul of liberty, there is, in fact, no liberty without it.

Frances Wright

Gender equality is more than a goal in itself. It is a precondition for meeting the challenge of reducing poverty, promoting sustainable development and building good governance.

Kofi Annan

October 26

Possessions

To the hobos, I'm imprisoned by everything I own.

Leon Russell

Looking at ourselves from the other side.

We imagine that because they have nothing, they envy us and long for possessions. And yes, you see the ones pushing a shopping trolley with all their worldly goods. They are protecting them lest they lose a part of themselves. The hobo, who has the clothes he stands in and a bench for a bed, has a freedom that we cannot even entertain. He can go wherever he likes without restraint.

Are we not all the same?

It's just that our trolley is more elegant than theirs. We guard it ferociously and constantly add new rubbish to it.

What can we leave at the side of the road today to make our journey lighter?

And don't forget to sift through the mental garbage we also lug along.

Anything you cannot relinquish when it has outlived its usefulness possesses you. And in this materialistic age, a great many of us are possessed by our possessions.

Peace Pilgrim

October 27

Now

If it is out of your hands, it deserves freedom from your mind too.

Ivan Nuru

How we torment ourselves. Drowning in the past or the future.

Replaying or scheming.

Uselessly.

Tormenting ourselves.

'Is there anything I can do about it now?' It is such a good question.

And when there is nothing we can do, we can make an appointment with ourselves in the future, when we may be able to do something about it and let it go.

Let it go.

Don't think about it.

Be here. In the now.

Be.

Even the smallest shift in perspective can bring about the greatest healing.

Joshua Kai

Emotions

Embrace all emotions: sadness, happiness, sorrow, hate, love, prejudice, fear; they are weapons against our greatest enemy: indifference.

Dave Matthes

A day without laughter is a day wasted.

Charlie Chaplin

Laugh.
Laugh out loud.
Cry.
Let your emotions out.
Let them bubble, pour out of you.
Do not repress them or yourself.
Open yourself to the world and enjoy yourself.
So many people live half-lives, controlling themselves and stifling their inner being.
Let go.
Become free.
Live.
Enjoy.

The emotion that can break your heart is sometimes the very one that heals it.

Nicholas Sparks

October 29

Adventure

Hello universe. Here I am. Now what will we get up to today.

Tony Brady

I have just done the meditation on Insight Timer in which Tony Brady asks this question. Or rather, he asked me.

And I, in turn, suggest that you ask it. Ask the universe and yourself.

How often do we go through the day, week, or month without ever considering what we will get up to?

How sad.

How belittling.

How diminishing.

Go out. Ask. Listen. Act. Enjoy.

Be fulfilled.

Because in the end, you won't remember the time you spent in the office or mowing the lawn. Climb that goddamn mountain.

Jack Kerouac

Procrastination

*Regret for the things we did can be tempered by time; it is regret for things we did **not** do that is inconsolable.*

Sydney Harris

Why do we put things off? Have you ever considered the time and energy you waste putting things off? Not to mention the pain.

Let's think about it. A letter arrives, and we think, not now. We push it aside. That's a minute of our lives wasted. Then, over the course of the next month, we see it and ignore it again. Feeling quietly bad.

Suddenly, we've accumulated thirty minutes of blackness because we haven't done what will probably only take us four or five minutes to do. And we still have them to come.

Bah.

If only we were cunning enough to do it straight away. Or have a slot once a week when we clear the backlog.

Such freedom.

Surely, nobody would continue to put it off.

Procrastination is like a credit card: it's a lot of fun until you get the bill.

Christopher Parker

Pause

He who can no longer pause to wonder and stand rapt in awe, is as good as dead; his eyes are closed.

Albert Einstein

We cannot think about more than one thing at a time. True, there are times when it feels as if we are thinking masses of stuff all at once, but if we explore the process more deeply, we'll realise there is only one thought at a time.

And what is interesting is that there is a pause between one thought leaving and another arriving.

If we are clever (and we are, very), we can become aware of the pause and go into it. In there is peace.

If we are clever, we can expand the pause, make it longer, larger. We can learn with practice, to dwell in the pause.

Such peace.

We are then so much better equipped to deal with the next thought when it comes.

Sometimes, you need to press pause to let everything sink in.

Sebastian Vettel

Enjoy
sharing
it
with
someone
else

November 1

Emotions

All emotions, even those that are suppressed and unexpressed, have physical effects. Unexpressed emotions tend to stay in the body like small ticking time bombs – they are illnesses in incubation.

Marilyn Van M Derbur

Oh dear.

All those times, we have pushed our feelings down and bitten our lip instead of letting out our anger, disappointment, jealousy or love and affection.

A ticking time bomb or slow-release poison?

We want to learn to let it out, not by erupting with violent emotion but by saying respectfully what we genuinely feel.

We want to learn to let it out and discover that the world doesn't end when we do. We go on. It goes on. And the world is richer because we dare to expose our feelings.

When negative feelings are suppressed, positive feelings become suppressed as well, and love dies.

John Gray

The dew of compassion is a tear.

Lord Byron

Anyone can tell you think you know me well. But you don't know me.

Cindy Walker / Eddy Arnold

November 2

Control

You cannot always control what goes on outside. But you can always control what goes on inside.

Wayne Dyer

The people in our lives are teachers. Nothing more. That is more than enough. How easily we forget this – if indeed we ever knew.

And so it makes sense that we realise we do not control them. We are not meant to.

Of course, the fact that we have spent most of our lives trying to do so makes it hard to let go.

You may think, 'Hang on, I never tried to control him/her.' 'He was my boss.' 'I knew I could never control him/her...'

Passive or submissive behaviour has an element of control, too.

We can control only one person, and that's difficult enough. That is ourselves.

Letting go of other people, letting them get on with their lives, and embracing them (mentally) with love enables us the freedom to embrace ourselves with love.

We can then steer our life in the right direction, in peace and harmony with ourselves.

By no longer trying to control others, we can help them when they come to us.

You cannot control what happens to you, but you can control your attitude to what happens to you, and in that, you will be mastering change, rather than allowing it to master you.

Brian Tracy

November 3

Being

In today's rush, we all think too much – seek too much – want too much – and forget about the joy of just being.

Eckhart Tolle

We do so much on autopilot. We tear through the day, never stopping to notice, never stopping to be.

Our ego yakking away, filling us with noise, deafness and blindness.

We want to retrain ourselves to start noticing, to start being present.

Walk across the room and, feel each step, look at a leaf. Study it. If you haven't got a leaf, look at the material of the top you are wearing. Look at the back of your hand, feel it, and be amazed by it. Listen to all the sounds around you. Put your hands on your chest and feel your heartbeat. Focus on your breath, in and out.

Be present.

Tell someone you love them.

Tell yourself you love you.

Be in the world.

Be present.

The present moment is filled with joy and happiness. If you are attentive, you will see it.

Thich Nhat Hanh

The moment is not found by seeking it, but by ceasing to escape from it.

James Pierce.

November 4

Emotions

In order to move on, you must understand why you felt what you did, and why you no longer need to feel it.

Mitch Albom

We create our feelings and emotions in other people.
Other people create their feelings and emotions in us.
Obvious, isn't it?

See two angry, sad or happy people together, and you can see feelings and emotions escalating.

But it works on all the feelings and emotions all the time, unless one of the people refuses to continue and changes the cycle.

So, if you are with anyone who is suffering in any way, the chances are that you are both reinforcing the suffering unless one of you refuses to accept the other's feelings.

Unless you do that, you enable them to feed their suffering.

We want to break the cycle.

We want to learn to live in peace and not allow them to pull us into their little hell.

That is the only way we can help them.

The best way out is always through.

Robert Frost

November 5

Wounds

*There are wounds that never show on the body, that are
deeper and more hurtful than anything that bleeds.*

Laurell K Hamilton

When our body is damaged, wounded, or hurt in any way,
we protect it and react instantly when anything or anyone
touches it.

Our mental wounds are the same. We guard them, and
when they are assaulted, we retaliate with anger, with attack
thoughts.

When something happens, we often go straight to the
attack thought without even processing why we feel like that.

It makes sense to use our sudden reactions as clues, as
signposts to what lies beneath them.

Slow everything down. Look inside and acknowledge the
source. And then do whatever we need to do to change that.

*Don't allow your wounds to transform you into someone
you are not.*

Paulo Coelho

*Our wounds are often the openings into the best and most
beautiful part of us.*

David Richo

November 6

Hiding

Man is not what he thinks he is, he is what he hides.

André Malraux

Fear is an illusion. We create it, or rather, our ego creates it in us as a way to control and isolate us from the world.

We put up barriers that we are, for the most part, unaware of.

If we can be open with others, and by that, I don't mean pouring out all our wickedness, real or imagined. I mean opening our heart. Saying at some deeper level, 'Here I am. I am here for you. I have not come to judge you. I am just here with you.'

When we do that, our fear evaporates. We are in the present with them. We are open. We are exchanging unconditional love.

It's good.

Do it.

It doesn't bite.

Shall I tell you the secret of the whole world? It is that we have only known the back of the world. We see everything from behind, and it looks brutal. That is not a tree but the back of a tree. That is not a cloud but the back of a cloud. Cannot you see that everything is stooping and hiding a face? If we could only get round in front.

G K Chesterton

Overwhelm

I tried to drown my sorrows, but the bastards learned how to swim, and now I am overwhelmed by this decent and good feeling.

Frida Kahlo

Sometimes, everything is overwhelming. It feels as if the heavens have opened and dumped all the rain as one solid block straight onto us. We are drowning in the mayhem of the moment.

It feels as if we must either accept it all and drown, or come out fighting and attacking everything and everyone – such pain.

But that is just our perception. We know that this is not real, that the rain always falls in drops. There is a way out.

We know that. But we forget it. We need to be reminded. We need to remind ourselves.

We almost certainly want to get away from the situation and look at it with some degree of calmness.

It will pass.

Everything passes.

That is the only certainty in the universe.

I noticed every time I felt overwhelmed, I would hold my breath. I had to learn to stop, relax and take long deep breaths, and within seconds, I would feel more clear and ready to deal with the situation in a more loving way.

Gisele Bündchen

November 8

Lessons

Everyone you meet has something to teach you.

Linda O Bella

That is <u>Everyone</u>.

Somehow, that changes everything. It changes the way we perceive the world.

If 'they' are here to teach 'me' something, I am therefore here to teach them something. So, our encounter changes, it has a meaning.

Whatever it is we are going through is a learning experience.

We are here to learn

Sometimes, we may hate the lesson, but isn't that how life is?

Ups and downs.

Good and bad.

Let us accept our lessons with love and return love, teach love, peace and calm.

I am always doing that which I cannot do, in order that I may learn how to do it.

Pablo Picasso

November 9

Growth

We should not judge people by their peak of excellence, but by the distance they have travelled from the point where they started.

Henry Ward Beecher

If we become, or when we become, the big fish in a small pond, we stop growing. We are limited. Our life starts to close in on us.

The only way to grow and achieve fulfilment is to always move to bigger ponds. To be challenging ourselves to be a small fish in a big pond, to learn mastery so that we can move on to the next pond and the one beyond.

The moment we rest on our laurels, we begin to die.

You are today, now, either growing or dying. Which do you choose?

Decide.

A bad day for your ego is a great day for your soul.

Jillian Michaels

November 10

Equality

A man does what he can; a woman does what a man cannot.

Isabel Allende

I sit here, looking at the river outside my window. Boats pass. And I wondered one day, how often do women steer them, so I started counting.

Six of the last one hundred boats to pass that had both men and women aboard had women at the helm.

If they are travelling east, there is a lock about two hundred yards ahead. You might argue that the men (the better?) helmsman should be at the wheel because they will have to go alongside.

But if he is at the helm, the woman must jump ashore with the line and tie them to the bollard.

I suspect most of them never even think about it or discuss it. Man, the competent master and woman, the slave.

And you, and me for that matter, do we make assumptions about our roles with the opposite sex without discussion?

Why?

I have not lived as a woman. I have lived as a man. I've just done what I've damn well wanted to, and I've made enough money to support myself and ain't afraid of being alone.

Katherine Hepburn

Lessons

Life is a succession of lessons which must be lived to be understood. All is riddle, and the key to a riddle is another riddle.

Ralph Waldo Emerson

There are people in our lives that we are meant to meet. There are lessons that we are here to learn. Some of them are more palatable than others.

Often, we meet people and we aren't willing to learn what we need to, during our interaction with them.

But this does not matter, and the lesson will be repeated with other people, in different situations, until we finally accept it.

We are here to grow and help others to grow. Whether we know or accept that.

If we approach life openly, we will have a smoother, more enjoyable journey.

Lessons are not given, they are taken.

Cesare Pavese

November 12

Help

Successful people are always looking for opportunities to help others. Unsuccessful people are always asking, 'What's in it for me?'

Brian Tracy

When I was about five years old, my Godmother, Elizabeth, came for a weekend. I took her for an adventure in the woods. After we had been going for forty-five minutes, we started to return, and I said, 'And now carry me'.

I don't remember this, of course – but she does. She has no children of her own. But carry me, she did.

As a five-year-old, it was easy to ask for help.

It is sad that, as grown-ups, we find it hard to ask for help.

And perhaps, doubly sad because it feels so good when others ask us for help, and we give it.

(Most of the time.)

Sometimes, the loudest cries for help are silent.

Harlan Coben

Asking for help is never a sign of weakness. It's one of the bravest things you can do. And it can save your life.

Lily Collins

November 13

Yes

If someone offers you an amazing opportunity, but you're not sure you can do it, say yes – then learn how to do it later.

Richard Branson

'Yes' or 'No'.

Which way do you lean naturally? It may depend, of course, on which of the lunatics in your life is saying, 'Do you want to...' Or 'Why don't we...'

But leaving aside the person speaking to us, we have a natural inclination to say yes or no.

Some of us have a 'Yes', followed almost immediately with the thought, 'Oh, what have I done'? Say, 'No!' and then, 'How can you get out of this?'

Many more of us have an automatic 'No'. Or a 'Let me think about that.' Followed by an internal, 'How can I say no to this?'

How boring life becomes if we only eat the same food day after day. Even if we don't realise how boring it is.

It is so good to encourage ourselves to lean toward 'Yes' and have adventures and excitement in our lives.

i imagine that yes is the only living thing

e e cummings

Say yes. To your internal joy. To self-love. To your internal strength, happiness and abundance. Each of these qualities will multiply every time you say 'Yes'.

Purvi Raniga

November 14

Patience

Patience is the best remedy for every trouble.

Plautus

We have struggles. Things have happened to us that we haven't planned, and we would not have chosen.

(If you are going through one now – patience, please.)

Despite all the unplanned things, we are here. We've made it through. And 99% of us are either better off or better people because of the things we have gone through.

Travelling through difficulties improves us. And it also makes us of more use to the world because we now have experience that we can use to share with and help others.

And so, going back to those of you who are waiting patiently – patience is the key. While we are suffering and battling our way through our overwhelming difficulties, please remember that others have overcome worse things, and have patience as you look beyond your current troubles. They will pass. Everything does.

One minute of patience, ten years of peace.

Greek Proverb

Patience is not simply the ability to wait – it's how we behave while we're waiting.

Joyce Meyer

November 15

Limitless

I can change. I can live out of my imagination instead of my memory. I can tie myself to my limitless potential instead of my limiting past.

Stephen R Covey

I just finished a meditation on 'Insight Timer' by JuneB called 'Welcome A Brand New Day'.

One of its affirmations, which struck a massive chord with me, is 'I am limitless'.

I am limitless.

So powerful. Such an all-encompassing statement. So full of power and promise. The gateway to whatever I want.

I am limitless.

Thank you.

We are spiritual beings whether we want to admit it or not, and inherent in our DNA is a design to return us home – home to our true essence, our greatest self, our limitless self.

Debbie Ford

November 16

Gratitude

'Is the spring coming?' he said. 'What is it like...?'
'It is the sun shining on the rain and the rain falling on the
sunshine...'

Francis Hodgson Burnett

And with the spring comes hope. The tiniest green shoot spearing its way out of the earth as it extends its life, filled with hope, into the air.

Hope draws us forward with anticipation and fills us with life.

Sometimes, it seems to fade, become less than, and disappears into worry and fear. The very idea of getting up and doing anything is just too much.

The solution, the way we re-awaken hope, is to bathe in gratitude.

Think of things you feel grateful for and let the feeling flood your body. Gratitude is not words, it is emotion spreading through you. And from it comes hope, pushing its green life out of the dark earth.

Embrace it, nurture it, and believe in it. Even if you do not fully understand what it is. Let it dance its magic through your being.

Hope is the thing with feathers that perches in the soul and sings the tune without the words and never stops at all.

Emily Dickinson

You cannot swim for new horizons until you have courage to lose sight of the shore.

William Faulkner

Learning

Do not take life too seriously. You will never get out of it alive.

Elbert Hubbard

If you want your child to listen, try talking softly to someone else.

Ann Landers

It is said that we need to hear, read, or be presented with new ideas seven times before we take them on board.

Some people say it is 21 times, but let's stick with seven.

So, if we want to get a new idea into someone else's head, we're going to want to repeat it seven times in one form or another.

An ideal way to achieve this is to find seven different ways to say the same thing.

We may want to think here about not nagging.

Nagging:- 'Put your plates in the dishwasher' after every meal frustrates and irritates them.

It is better to sit down and discuss the plate and dishwasher with them so that they can take responsibility for it.

And when we think, 'I've heard this before', do not discard the message. Instead, think, 'Hooray, I must be learning'.

You never really learn much from hearing yourself speak.

George Clooney

November 18

Living

Every man dies. Not every man really lives.

William Ross Wallace

What are you going to do about it?

I don't know you from Adam, And if I'm going to be completely honest, I don't know Adam either.

But it is so easy to slip into the habit of the same old, same old. I know. I do it, too.

And it is good to remind ourselves to get off our bums and do something with our lives.

Good luck.

Enjoy.

Life should not be a journey to the grave with the intention of arriving safely in a pretty and well-preserved body, but rather to skid broadside in a cloud of smoke, thoroughly used up, totally worn out, and loudly proclaiming 'Wow! What a ride!'

Hunter S Thompson

Procrastination

If you want to conquer fear, don't sit at home and think about it. Go out and get busy.

Dale Carnegie

Yesterday, we published our second book. And I feel so alive with excitement. Thinking about it, I realise we could have finished it a good while ago. And it was just fear that prevented us. Fear slowed us down, and we found extra things to do.

Fear of what? Failure? Or just a quiet, nameless fear that prevents forward motion.

I mention this because I do not think we are unique in this fear. I suspect that many of us do it without even realising it. We push the end, the completion of something away.

Maybe if we were really clever, we could recognise this and not do it again?

There is no failure except in no longer trying.

Elbert Hubbard

Success is not final, failure is not fatal. It is the courage to continue that counts.

Winston Churchill

November 20

Alignment

Power is when what you think, say and do align.

Richie Norton

How do you behave when no one is watching?
Is it different?
If it is, then we are damaging ourselves.

We have, at our core, a knowing, a standard, and when we violate it, we lessen ourselves.

We want to be in alignment with ourselves – mind, body and soul.

It empowers us. We are, then, better in whatever situation we are in.

When your passions and desires align, you cannot hold them back.

M F Moonzajer

November 21

Choices

You are always responsible for how you act, no matter how you feel.

Robert Tew

It's not that I've been invited to the hole I am standing in. It's that I accepted the invitation.

Craig D Lounsbrough

Throughout our lives, we have made choices.

Choices about our behaviours, our beliefs, our role in society, our role in our relationships, and our abilities. And many of them we simply go along with today, believing that we cannot change them.

And just reading that, without going into depth about any of them, we realise that we can change them if we decide to.

We do not need to continue to be the person we have presented to the world all these years. And we do not need to stick to the choice we made yesterday, last week, or last month.

Yes, change is scary. It is always frightening.

Often, we stay stuck, being treated in ways that are at some level disrespectful, if not abusive.

Just because we have always washed his clothes doesn't mean we must continue doing so. Just because we have always done anything doesn't mean we have to continue doing it.

We can make a new choice. That is what it means to be human. To have the ability to choose what we do and be free.

Good behaviour is the last refuge of mediocrity.

Henry S Haskins

Can you remember who you were, before the world told you who you should be?

Charles Bukowski

November 22

Resentments

'Resentment – Bitter indignation at being treated unfairly.'

Oxford Dictionary

Ah yes. Resentments. Now that's something we can really get our teeth into. Make a meal of.

And actually, most resentments don't come close to being bitter indignations. By and large, they are just a collection of all the slights people have or haven't said or done.

'He bumped into me.' 'She didn't say that my top looked good.' 'They had more than me...' blah blah.

Often, they have no idea that you think they've done something wrong.

The only person we are hurting with any resentment is ourselves.

Forgiveness and resentment cannot co-exist.

Could there be a clue there?

And please let us start by forgiving ourselves for everything we have done.

Forgiveness opens the door to freedom.

Open your eyes and see what you can with them, before they close forever.

Anthony Doerr

November 23

Behaviour

Wrong is wrong, even if everyone is doing it. Right is right, even if no one is doing it.

Ralph Waldo Emerson

Daffodils are growing by the river outside my window. This morning, a girl about four and her younger brother ran up to them.

She got there first, and she knelt to smell them. Her brother charged along and kicked at one as hard as he could. (I was quietly pleased when his foot missed the flower, and he landed on his back.)

So there you have it. Both are surely too young to have been indoctrinated with those behaviours.

Thank God for women, I say.

No child is ever born afraid. Fear is learned behaviour.

Cherie Carter-Scott

November 24

Manipulation

You can't manipulate people who know how to think for themselves.

Trish Mercier

Mrs Hopewell had no bad qualities of her own, but she was able to use other people's in such a constructive way that she never felt the lack.

Flannery O'Connor

So here's the thing – you're a vegetarian. (If you aren't, bear with me and pretend, you can stop being one again in a few minutes.) You're a vegetarian and have friends, family members, and work colleagues who are not.

You sit down and eat with them, and they eat the most delicious steak. The very best, not from a supermarket but bought from a real farm.

They go on and on about how you really should try it. If you loved them, you would. If you want to keep your job, you would. If you want them to go on doing 'all' those things for you, you would. If you want to go on seeing your children, you would.

'Look, it's just a small piece of meat. I cut it, especially for you. You used to love it. Go on, eat it. *Please*. Just for me. Just to keep me happy.'

Know anyone like that?

Do you ever do that to anyone?

So?

Are you trying to manipulate me? It's working.

Bridget Moynahan

November 25

Being

All the wonders you seek are in yourself. We should seek to discover our own special light.

Fyodor Tyutchev

Our light is there. Always. We can claim it.

We can live in our days with it. We can view the world through it. We can react to the world with it.

It is possible to stop being dominated by our ego.

It is possible to think and react with love. And with peace.

All the wonders you seek are within yourself, and when you live with them, you spread the wonder out into the world.

And you are there, open, able to receive wonder from the world.

In your soul lives a whole world of mysterious and enchanted thoughts; they will be drowned by the noise of this world. Be still and listen to their singing and be silent.

Fyodor Tyutchev

Talking

A fool is made more of a fool when their mouth is more open than their mind.

Anthony Liccione

Trust your mind when it says it has nothing much to say.

Michael Bassey Johnson

What do you say when someone asks how are you?

It seems there are four general responses. "I'm fine, thanks." Which really means, "F**k off and leave me alone".

Then there's 'I'm okay, but...' and some detail about oneself.

Then there's the response that pukes all their problems, real or imagined, and they fall into the category, "Don't ask Mary how she is, she'll tell you!"

Finally, there is a genuine response about how one is, but this one only wants to be given to a trusted friend.

When people ask you how you are, most of them are not interested, so don't bore them.

It's probably worth looking at which is your default response and consider if you want to change it.

So wearied was I by the long-winded account of his illness, I fell asleep, only to awake and hear myself say, 'And did you die?'

Enid Evans

November 27

Thoughts

What others think about you is none of your business.

Jack Canfield

There they are, thinking about you, or perhaps they aren't. Is that even worse?

But whether they are or not, if it is none of your business, then it doesn't matter.

The fact that it is none of your business is liberating. It allows you to get on with being your best you, without worry.

It is so draining if we go through our life constantly doing, being, and behaving in the hope that it will meet with their approval and praise.

Let go of it.

Oh, and as a side benefit, stop constantly analysing everything they do. It is such a waste of energy.

Live your life.

Enjoy

Usually, people who ask, 'Do you know who I am?' Don't have a clue themselves.

Christina Engela

November 28

Stopping

Doing nothing often leads to the very best of something.

A A Milne

There are days when our mind and body withdraw from the world and appear to be desperate to shut down.

If we have things that we 'have to do,' the chances are that we will do them, but not nearly as well as the days when we feel empowered.

If we have a choice, if it is possible, it is a better idea to take some time off. To allow our mind and body to shut down so that we can reboot it into excellence.

We may only need to shut down for a few minutes or an hour. Sometimes, we may really need a day. But if we can give ourselves permission to stop, rest and restart, everyone will benefit.

Taking time to do nothing often brings everything into perspective.

Doe Zantamata

November 29

Knowledge

*Comfortable in the knowledge that everything is
temporary.*

Angela Hughes

It is so easy to forget the temporary nature of everything
when we are totally 'in' what is happening in our lives.

It may not even be manifesting 24 hours a day. We may
enjoy having periods of respite from it.

But when we return to 'it', we forget the peace. 'It'
consumes us so completely that it feels as if it is happening
24/7.

And even if we can vaguely hope/believe that 'it' will not
go on forever, it feels impossible to imagine the future
without it.

But everything is temporary.

In case you didn't get that, 'Everything is temporary.'

So take a breath, and begin to realise, to believe that.

Oh, and I feel measly mentioning this, but the good
things in our lives are temporary too.

*Life is a gift... Life is a test... Life is a temporary
assignment.*

Rick Warren

*When you are lost in the dark, remember the darkness of
the night, and how it helps to make the stars shine.*

Michael Bassey Johnson

November 30

Enjoyment

Love what you do, otherwise you won't make a success of it.

Anne-Marie Dyas

I read the above quote and wrote it out, only I changed it to 'love what you do, otherwise you won't make a difference'.

And I guess for me, making a difference is what's important. No, actually, what is important is loving what you do.

So many of us have jobs because that is what we do.

I once worked as a stockbroker in my twenties for three years. Then I left. And since then, although I have done many different things, I have just enjoyed myself.

So important to enjoy oneself. It is essential to choose to change the way we view things so that we enjoy them.

Go forth and enjoy your life.

There is joy in work. There is no happiness except in the realisation that we have accomplished something.

Henry Ford

Forgive

Completely

December 1

Equality

A lie doesn't become truth, wrong doesn't become right, and evil doesn't become good, just because it's accepted by a majority.

Booker T Washington

Let's leave aside the world's problems for a moment and think about our own.

Are we pulling our weight at home, at work, in the world, or are we doing much more than others?

And thinking, 'Well, that's just the way it is,' 'That's the way it's always been,' or 'There's nothing I can do about it' is just a cop-out.

We can do more – if we want to.

Or we can refuse to be taken advantage of.

If you are burdened with guilt or resentment because of what is happening in your life, there is something wrong.

Peel away the layers honestly, look at it, and change it.

Dare to live.

We will never have true civilisation until we have learned to recognise the rights of others.

Will Rogers

Men are from Earth, women are from Earth, deal with it.

George Carlin

I am free of all prejudices. I hate everyone equally.

W C Fields

December 2

Struggle

We draw our strength from the very despair in which we have been forced to live. We shall endure.

Cesar Chavez

The bravest thing I ever did was continuing my life when I wanted to die.

Juliette Lewis

There are moments when the blackness descends, surrounding us. The pain and despair can feel totally insurmountable. It can completely fill the future, with no hint or hope of light beyond it.

You may say, 'Well, that hasn't happened to me.'

It has happened to me, although now, searching back through my life, I find it difficult to pinpoint it.

And yet, if I look back at the struggles, the awfulness in my life, here I am. I have come through.

And because of that, I am more complete and have more abilities to give to the world and myself.

And so.

This too shall pass. The bad and the good.

When we can, we want to feel gratitude for both.

Life begins on the other side of despair.

Jean-Paul Sartre

Action is the antidote to despair.

Joan Baez

December 3

Meditation

Being hot never hurts.

Debbie Harry

Very foolishly, I was travelling on the London Underground on the hottest day of the year. I did not have a seat. It felt as if I was standing in a puddle of sweat.

Just as we began to leave the station, the train juddered to a standstill. (Oh, by the way, the London Underground does not have air-con.)

And there we stayed, for over twenty minutes, with all the doors closed while the guards trotted up and down inside the train.

Someone had pulled the handle to stop the train!

It was possible to feel the anger as it bounced from one passenger to the next. Apparently, the man had left his phone on the platform. So naturally, he pulled the handle. That's what one does, isn't it?

I only tell you this heartwarming tale as a thank you to meditation. After the first minute or two of allowing my irritation to bubble towards anger, I said to myself, 'No,' and I started to meditate.

I removed myself from the insanity of the situation and went into peace. I could still feel the sweat trickle down my body, but I viewed that as gentle entertainment.

We have a choice as to how we react in any situation.

We are all on mastering our inner peace.

Raheem DeVaughn

December 4

Doing

The most important job in life is to find out the purpose of your life, and go for it wholeheartedly.

Debases Mirdha

Whatever we are doing, we want to do it fully. We want to give it our attention and embrace it with our being.

That is the way to live and be alive. That is what ignites every part of ourselves, physical, mental, and spiritual.

If we are doing things half-heartedly or when we give up something, part of us is dying. We are shrivelling up physically, mentally and spiritually.

You know the difference you feel when you are doing something to get by and when you are totally committed to doing anything with enthusiasm. And the way that you feel is manifesting its way throughout you.

Choose to live

Choose to live completely. Choose to live a long and joy-filled life.

A boy carries out suggestions more wholeheartedly when he understands their aim.

Robert Baden-Powell

December 5

Blame

A man can fail many times, but he isn't a failure until he begins to blame somebody else.

John Burroughs

So easy to blame. It is so easy to find fault outside oneself.

After all, it's such a natural thing to do. Something goes wrong, and we instantly look for the reason, and if anyone else is involved, it is easy to blame them.

Even to the extent that if we drop something on our foot, it's their fault because they asked us to move.

Blame is a cancer.

If invited in, it grows and spreads through our being, poisoning us and poisoning everyone else.

Take responsibility for everything you do or say, even if you are doing it because they asked you.

Take responsibility for your life.

Take pride in the way you do things.

The best years in your life are the ones in which you decide your problems are your own. You do not blame them on your mother, the ecology or the president. You realise that you control your own destiny.

Albert Ellis

Life

Life isn't about finding yourself. Life is about creating yourself.

George Bernard Shaw

It's so easy to overcomplicate everything and end by doing much less than we might because we spend more time thinking than doing.

So here are a couple of simple ideas that make life wonderful.

The first is to be a good person. That's it, be a good person.

The second is to do a job that you love. Do something that fulfils you.

If you don't love your job at the moment, then love everything you can about it. Identify the positives in it and focus on them. Even if it's the inadequate money you get from it. Find some way to view it positively. And use that to enable you to do something that you do love, whenever you can.

Focus on the positives. Have gratitude.

He who has a why to live can bear almost any how.

Frederick Nietzsche

You think people should be nice. They're not. They're just like you.

Anthony DeMello

December 7

Attention

Approach each task as if it were your last.

Marcus Aurelius

How often do you give your full attention to what you are doing?

Most of the time, our mind is not focused on what we are doing. It is flitting from one thing to another.

And while there may be no permanent cure for that, just being aware of it and devoting our attention to what we are doing makes a huge difference to how we feel and what we achieve.

Any man who can drive safely whilst kissing a pretty girl is simply not giving the kiss the attention it deserves.

Albert Einstein

Unconscious

Almost all of our mind is unconscious. We have to learn to communicate with that mysterious part of our mind.

Elsa Punset

A friend of mine, a hypnotherapist, saw two people fighting with knives. One of them stabbed the other and ran off.

My friend, let's call him John, dashed to the fallen man. The blood was squirting from an artery.

John, being a hypnotherapist, took the man's hand, looked into his eyes and commanded, 'STOP BLEEDING!' The message went straight to the man's unconscious, and the bleeding stopped.

When the ambulance arrived, paramedics told John that there was no way this man should still be alive. He should have bled to death by then.

Our unconscious can do truly amazing things if given the correct instructions.

We live in a culture that believes that most of what we do is consciously. However, most of what we do, and what we do best, is done unconsciously.

John Grinder

December 9

Faith

Anyone who has spent a few nights in a tent during a storm can tell you: the world doesn't care all that much if you live or die.

Anthony Doerr

In my twenties, I built a boat with a couple of friends. We sailed from the UK to The Canary Islands.

A couple of days after we left Tangiers, we were engulfed in a storm that lasted for nine days. (On the fifth day, the storm had a rest, and we thought it was over, but it wasn't.)

Most of the time, the winds were so strong that we had no sails up.

We saw no land or any other boat during those nine days. Occasionally, thank goodness we were on the top of a wave before tearing down its side into the trough between the waves.

To say 'It was all very frightening' does not even begin to express...

I understood why man had to believe in God. There was no other way he could survive.

Seeing death as the end of life is like seeing the horizon as the end of the ocean.

David Searls

If the ocean can calm itself, so can we. We are both salt water mixed with air.

Nayyirah Waheed

December 10

Social Media

Social Media is not a safe space.

Tarana Burke

It takes discipline not to let social media steal your time.

Alexis Ohanian

Do you use social media? Do you enjoy it? Is it essential in your life? Is it your friend?

Oh, and please don't tell me you only use it to keep track of your friend in Oz or your sister's son, who is travelling.

Next time... Before you open any of these platforms, take a moment to 'rate your feelings.'

And when you've finished looking at whatever you were looking at, 'rate your feelings' again.

Most of the time, if they are honest, most people feel less good about themselves after being on it.

The reason is simple, most of the stuff that people post is a lie. They present themselves and 'their day' in the best light, even when something isn't going well.

While we, poor humans, are left with ourselves and our shortcomings.

So the question really is, 'If it doesn't make me feel good, why am I doing it?'

And somehow, if we are honest, the answer is, 'Well, everyone is doing it. I'd be in the dark if I didn't,' or 'What would we talk about?' Are not really convincing arguments.

The more social media we have, the more we think we are connecting, yet we are really disconnecting from each other.

J R

December 11

Listening

Always listen to the warnings from your heart.

Teresa Collins

I woke up this morning, got up and started to dress when a wave of tiredness came over me and consumed my being. So I flopped back into bed, half-dressed, pulled up the covers and went back to sleep.

In fact, I only slept for another ten minutes before getting up again. But I needed every one of those minutes.

And so often, we deny ourselves our needs, charging on not listening to the messages we receive.

I believe that we suffer when we do not listen. We suffer, and we take that suffering into the world.

I am not just talking about grabbing some extra sleep. I am talking about listening to ourselves.

When your intuition speaks, listen. When your ego speaks, shut it up.

Dee Duncan

December 12

Addiction

In ancient times, cats were worshipped as gods; they have not forgotten this.

Terry Pratchett

I visited a castle in Scotland once owned by a pop star. He had a cat that used to love jumping off its roof.

If all the doors were open, it would dash to the top as quickly as it could and jump off. Fly down, land, and dash back to the roof again.

I thought it was both wonderful and strange.

I have since met many people with an extraordinary array of addictions, and by comparison, the cat's behaviour seems pretty tame.

And at least the cat was not hurting anyone.

It is good to be a cynic – it is better to be a contented cat – and it is best not to exist at all.

H P Lovecraft

December 13

Kindness

*You can never do a kindness too soon, for you never know
how soon it will be too late.*

Ralph Waldo Emerson

How often do we hesitate and forget? So easy to think,
'Oh yes, must do that...' And then life happens.

We forget. We don't even notice that we haven't. It has
been quietly swept from our mind.

What joy we feel when someone does the unexpected for
us. Or even the expected, the hoped for.

Maybe some tiny expression, perhaps three words, come
up but somehow fail to make it past our lips.

'I love you.'

'That's delicious.'

'You are amazing.'

'So special to be with you.'

*The only real things in life are the unexpected things.
Everything else is just an illusion.*

Watkin Tudor Jones

The finest of pleasures are always the unexpected ones.

Erin Morgenstern

December 14

Growth

Don't go through life, grow through life.

Eric Butterworth

There are sunflower competitions. Everyone is given a small sunflower in a little pot. Who can grow the tallest?

Lots of people leave it in the small pot for a few days. They never win. The small pot restricts its growth. It thinks small.

The winning sunflower is the one that is planted out at once. It is given freedom, watered, fed, tended and loved.

That is what it needs to win. And even if it is not quite as tall as the others, it is a winner.

Surely, the person who comes third in an Olympic final deserves as much praise as the person who wins.

Strive not to be a success but rather to be of value.

Albert Einstein

December 15

Practice

The one who learns and learns but doesn't practice is like the one who ploughs and ploughs but never plants.

Plato

Many people get lost in the planning. Planning, studying, and researching is their comfort zone. There is no risk involved. They excuse their lack of action with, 'I just need to understand this...'

And many people believe the old adage, 'Practice makes Perfect'. So they practice and practice without learning anything new or very little.

The truth is that practice makes permanent. It locks in all the mistakes we've learned. So we do want to practice, but we want to be open to new and different ideas. We want to challenge ourselves, and we want to live. We want to be alive.

Challenge yourself, it's the only path which leads to growth.

Morgan Freeman

December 16

Gratitude

Gratitude is riches. Complaint is poverty.

Doris Day

It is so easy to think or write down gratitude for the things in our lives without fully going into the feeling of gratitude.

This is like eating food without bothering to taste and savour it.

We cannot be grateful for more than one thing at a time.

We want to immerse ourselves in the gratitude for something, choose the first thing and feel the gratitude in every cell of our body.

Then, choose the next thing and feel gratitude for that.

Writing down what you are grateful for may be a helpful list.

But writing them down is pointless unless you stop long enough to actually, do the gratitude.

As we express our gratitude, we must never forget that the highest appreciation is not to utter words but to live by them.

John F Kennedy

December 17

Choice

Life is like a sandwich
Birth as one slice
And death as the other
What you put in between the slices is up to you.
Is your sandwich tasty or sour?

Allan Rufus

Our training started before we were born. Our mother's positive or negative outlook was already being drummed into us.

And so, as the days, weeks, and years passed, we developed our view of the world.

We either approached the world with openness and love or with fear and hostility.

Yes, there were variations, but ultimately, we lean towards a negative or positive view of the world. If you were unlucky enough to be weaned on criticism and pessimism, you probably still lean toward them unless you have already made changes in that area.

If we see other people as failures and assume they see us in the same way. What a depressing spiral.

Everything changes if we cultivate the habit of looking for the good in our lives and for the good in others.

I have a friend I see infrequently, who always finds something to compliment me on, my watch, my clothing, my laughter... It always makes me feel good.

Take baby steps and look for the good in the people you spend time with. Look for opportunities to compliment people.

Keep your face always toward the sunshine – and the
shadows will fall behind you.

Walt Whitman

December 18

Ego

The ego is the false self, born out of fear and defensiveness.

John O'Donohue

The ego relies on the familiar. It is reluctant to experience the unknown, which is the very essence of life.

Deepak Chopra

Our Ego is a bully. Loud. It's like a feral child who's eaten too much sugar at a birthday party. It wants to do everything it can to ensure we're enslaved. And, although it's hard to believe, it does not want us to succeed. It may lay out a trail of little rewards for us, but these are simply there to lead us to the next bad thing.

And standing ever so patiently and quietly in the wings, just waiting for us to call it and take over, is the solution. Call it your inner voice, god, your higher power, the holy spirit, or whatever you will, it is there.

And when we call it, it comes. Quietly and confidently, an inner knowing, a peace arrives. If we say, do this for me, and let go, it does, and we can move serenely forward.

The challenge is that as soon as we hand it over, the ego, equipped with a vast trunk of noisy explosive toys, rants and screams and does its best to get us to destroy our peace.

The good news is that the more often we hand our lives over to our quiet inner voice, the stronger it becomes and the easier it is to find and rely on.

Your inner voice is the voice of divinity. To hear it, we need to be in solitude, even in crowded places.

A R Rahman

December 19

Being

We need to find God, and he cannot be found in noise and restlessness. God is the friend of silence. See how nature – trees, flowers, grass – grows in silence. See the stars, the moon and the sun, how they move in silence... We need silence to be able to touch souls.

Mother Teresa

Listen to all the things you can't hear, the outside and the inside things.

I live by a river in the country, a magical place to walk, refresh, and lose oneself. People go by, and around 20% of them have their faces ensnared by their phones.

About another 20%, could be more (I can't always tell), it could be many more, have their headphones plugged in.

Why?

I just watched a deer saunter past, nibbling leaves from a tree. I am so very lucky.

It is through gratitude for the present moment that the spiritual dimension of life opens up.

Eckhart Tolle

December 20

Goals

Let your dreams devour your life, not your life devour your dreams.

Antoine de Saint-Exupéry

Many people who have a dream are like horses going over jumps. They may manage the first few, then comes a bigger one. The horse stops, the rider whizzes past its ears and crashes to the ground. (Weeping emoji face) and that's it. End of dream.

If that happens to you, re-group, re-evaluate. Look at everything. Focus, refocus. Grasp your dream and move on towards it. Be proud to be you. Focus. Do it.

Do not slide into oblivion.

Keep going. It is worth it, even if it's not what you expected.

Picking up the pieces of a shattered dream is better than having no pieces to pick up at all.

Matshona Dhliwayo

December 21

God

'Where is God? Where can I find him?' We ask. We don't realise that's like a fish swimming frantically through the ocean in search of the ocean.

Ted Dekker

There is only one God.

Accepting that makes everything so much easier. It means that all the people who appear to be following/worshipping other Gods are all praying to the same God. They have just put their own labels and stories to it.

And their egos have done their best to make them believe their way is the only way.

God is within each of us. We only need to go within to find it. It is there. And when we do that totally, all the conventions, external beliefs and rules disappear. There is God, and the wisdom and the peace are available to you.

I am not saying that there is anything wrong with your beliefs. It is just that God is boundless, beyond comprehension, simply wisdom, peace and love. There for everyone. There for all of us.

All that is real in me is God; all that is real in God is I. The gulf between God and me is thus bridged. Thus by knowing God, we find that the kingdom of heaven is within us.

Swami Vivekananda

December 22

Action

The secret to getting ahead is getting started.

Mark Twain

Although many people do not know it, we tend to fall into one of three groups, starters, finishers, and those that happily go along in the middle.

It is good to work out which we are. If you work with people, it's essential to have the right people doing the part of the job that naturally fills their tendency.

Many people find it challenging to start jobs. They don't know where to begin. The trick is to begin. If it's not the right place to start, it doesn't matter.

And if you have problems finishing things, travel beyond them in your mind, imagine your world a day or two after everything is done, and feel the sense of joy and accomplishment that comes with that.

The thing about finishing a story is that finishing is really only the beginning.

William Herring

December 23

Self-Indulgence

The self-indulgent man craves for all pleasant things... and is led by his appetite to choose these at the cost of everything else.

Aristotle

Those moments when you start to look around, feeling that you want something.

Quite likely food, drink, or maybe a drug. Perhaps a purchase. 'I need to buy something'.

Often, we get on with fulfilling the desire without even processing it. Suddenly, there is a whiskey, a cup of tea, or a doughnut in front of us, and we are consuming it.

I only mention this because there are about one and a half seconds between the initial idea and the first movement towards its obtainment.

Should we desire to change our habits, if we start to bookmark those one-and-a-half seconds, we can choose a different course of action when they appear.

Not easy, perhaps, but not impossible either.

Our soul is sometimes a king, sometimes a tyrant. An uncontrolled, over-indulgent soul is turned from king to the most feared tyrant.

Seneca

Anything worth doing is worth overdoing.

Mick Jagger

Too much of a good thing can be wonderful.

Mae West

December 24

Healing

We are born healers, and this is our superpower.

Helene Popescu

We are all healers. We all have the gift of healing. We are either giving, sending out healing and love, or we are not.

All the time.

Every interaction we have with others either benefits and heals them or it does not.

Every interaction we have with ourselves either benefits and heals us, or it does not.

Love and positivity heal.

Everything else damages.

Everything else poisons.

It is that simple.

'What happens when people open their hearts?' 'They get better.'

Haruki Murakami

December 25

Letting Go

Let go or be dragged.

Zen proverb

Intelligence consists in ignoring things that are irrelevant.

Nassim Nicholas Taleb

There is a story about two monks walking along. They come to a river. A beautiful young woman is there, hoping to cross the river. Despite his vows, one of the monks picks her up and carries her across. The two monks walk on. A mile or so later, the other monk says, 'You should not have done that!' the first monk replies, 'I carried her and left her there. You obviously have not!'

That's us, or most of us. We carry all the rubbish with us long after we should have moved on from it.

We want to learn to let go of things. Unclutter our minds and lives.

Look past your thoughts so you may drink the pure nectar of this moment.

Rumi

You can't throw the towel in and hang onto the corner of it.

William Crowley

December 26

Knowledge

Do not let the roles you play make you forget who you are.

Roy T Bennett

'Who are you?'

Most people, when asked that, or the similar, 'What do you do?' Answer by rote.

I'm a builder, a housewife, a salesman, a computer programmer, etc. All just meaningless labels. Not who you are at all.

It bears thinking about. It is worth considering, picking apart and discovering who you are and what you stand for and believe in.

It gives you clarity and purpose and frees you to confidently say what you think and believe.

What you have is momentary, who you are is forever.

Frank Sonnenberg

Self-Indulgent

Usually, I'm so self-absorbed that my companion could be bleeding to death and I might not notice.

Pamela Druckerman

It is easy to lose ourselves. Endlessly comparing ourselves to others as we wonder if we match up!

'How do I look?' 'Am I witty enough?' 'Do they admire me for what I say?' 'Is this what I'm supposed to say?

It is perhaps worth mentioning that as we listen to all the rubbish spouted by others, we cannot conceive that others are asking themselves these questions. But they probably are.

Of course while we judge ourselves (belittle ourselves?) while we are with others, we are not listening fully to what they are saying. We are not present.

Which is a shame, because we are with them to learn something. If only we would listen.

Relax; the world is not watching too closely. It's too busy contemplating itself in the mirror.

Richelle E Goodrich

December 28

Self-Judgement

Don't concern yourself with the opinions of those who judge you. That is placing on them an importance they do not have.

Donna Lynn Hope

We don't expect the people in our lives to be perfect. (We may wish they were, but we know with only a little thought that they never will be.)

We sometimes look at pictures of celebrities, and we may think their lives are perfect.

We may aspire to be like them.

We may judge our imperfections against their apparent success.

We may think that the other 'normal' people in our lives are doing much better than we are.

We may collect all our shortcomings, small and large and magnify them. Creating a vast 'less than' image of ourselves.

If we did any of these, we probably do them without any real thought, and our ego uses them all to find new and more devastating ways to belittle ourselves.

If we were to look at it from an unbiased viewpoint, we could realise that such self-persecution is just that, self-persecution.

Then, we might accept and like ourselves just as we are.

Wanting to be someone else is a waste of the person you are.

Marilyn Monroe

December 29

Fear

*Nothing in life is to be feared, it is only to be understood.
Now is the time to understand more, so that we may fear
less.*

Marie Curie

Sometimes, we feel fear and anxiety, and it's overwhelming and paralyses us. It picks up all our troubles and ties them together so they appear huge and seemingly inescapable.

And even if we know the main cause of our fear, it has collected so many others that we can no longer see any of them clearly.

Our first step out of that has to be to acknowledge fear.

Next, we want to peel back the layers and identify one fear. Just one, not necessarily the primary fear, but one thing troubling us, face it, deal with it. Do what needs to be done to change it. To remove it.

This loosens the mass of fear. Gives us a new perspective. And we can then, when we are ready, move on to the next fear.

We can confront things individually. As a mass, they overwhelm and destroy us.

*He who is not every day conquering some fear has not
learned the secret of life.*

Ralph Waldo Emerson

December 30

Reality

Reality is that which, when you stop believing in it, doesn't go away.

Philip K Dick

We create our own reality.

If you doubt this, a little reflection will make you realise it's true.

Think of the times you have greeted anyone with love, happiness and joy and received the same in return.

Think of the times you have gone out feeling grumpy, angry, frightened, and the world has responded to you with blackness in one form or another.

You were creating your reality.

So we have a choice.

And if we greet the world with gratitude and love, if we share that with the world, it will respond with gratitude, love and abundance.

But I know, somehow, that only when it is dark enough can you see the stars.

Martin Luther King Jnr

December 31

Expectations

Thoughts don't become things; thoughts ARE things.

Eric Michael Leventhal

I hope your day is better than you expect.
And what would that be like?
If you knew?
Most of the time, we go through our day with little expectation.

If, before the day unfolds, we spend some time going through, painting it the way we would like it to be, it's more likely to manifest that way.

Not much of an effort for vast rewards.

The universe is not outside of you. Look inside yourself; everything that you want, you already have.

Rumi